Sweet Ideas
FROM
EQUAL®
SWEETENER WITH

NutraSweet®
BRAND SWEETENER

PUBLICATIONS INTERNATIONAL, LTD.

Photography: Sanders Studios, Inc., Chicago

Pictured on the front cover: Cherry Lattice Pie *(page 44).*

Pictured on the back cover *(top to bottom):* Strawberry Smoothie *(page 8),* Orange Jubilee *(page 10),* Blueberry Triangles *(page 72),* Chicken and Fruit Salad *(page 38)* and Rich Chocolate Cheesecake *(page 62).*

ISBN: 0-7853-2398-8

Manufactured in U.S.A.

8 7 6 5 4 3 2 1

Microwave Cooking: Microwave ovens vary in wattage. The microwave cooking times given in this publication are approximate. Use the cooking times as guidelines and check for doneness before adding more time. Consult manufacturer's instructions for suitable microwave-safe cooking dishes.

Questions about Equal®? Call toll-free 1-800-323-5316, hours 8 a.m. to 5 p.m. CST. Or write to Equal® Consumer Affairs, Benevia, Suite 900, The Merchandise Mart, 200 World Trade Center Chicago, Chicago, Illinois 60654.

Sweet Ideas FROM EQUAL SWEETENER WITH NutraSweet BRAND SWEETENER

EQUAL®

Sweet Facts

It's been over a decade since Americans were invited to experience the sweet life with Equal®, the tasty sweetener from The NutraSweet Company, which has all the great taste of sugar and only a fraction of the calories. Since then, Equal sweetener has revolutionized the way we eat and has become an American classic . . . because it's in a class by itself.

It's easy to make Equal a part of your daily diet. Just about anyone who cares about good taste and maintaining a healthful lifestyle enjoys Equal. For years, Equal has been available in packet and tablet forms. And recently, we've introduced our product in two new bulk forms—Equal® Measure™ and Equal® Spoonful™. You don't have to open packet after packet to cook and bake with Equal® sweetener.

Equal® Measure™ is the same concentrated product that has been making life sweet for almost 15 years—but in a package that's easier to use with your favorite Equal recipes. Every large pouch of Equal Measure has the same sweetening power as 57 Equal packets or one pound of sugar. And granulated Equal® Spoonful™ (formerly NutraSweet® Spoonful™), the newest addition to our product line, measures just like sugar. As you can see, these forms are ideal for recipes and pitcher drinks. So, it's really easy to make Equal a part of your daily diet.

Sweet Ideas from Equal® offers 72 flavorful, healthful recipes for your enjoyment. Recipes range from beverages, salads and entrées to a tempting variety of desserts. But keep in mind, baking without sugar can be tricky.* Equal sweetens like sugar, but its cooking properties are different. We've created these new versions of your favorite recipes, specially designed to let you bake successfully with Equal.

You'll find essential nutrition information with every recipe. We've calculated the nutrition values using the basic recipe without garnishes or optional ingredients. When ingredient choices appear in the recipe, we've used the first choice for the nutrition analysis. If you have diabetes or follow the Exchange Lists for Meal Planning, you'll want to note the Food Exchanges listed with each recipe. Like the other nutrition information, these are based on the basic recipe without garnishes or optional ingredients. The Food Exchanges have been rounded to the nearest half number.

EQUAL® EQUIVALENT SWEETNESS CHART

Sugar	Equal® Packets	Equal® Measure™*	Equal® Spoonful™
2 tsp.	1	¼ tsp. (approx.)	2 tsp.
1 Tbsp.	1½	½ tsp.	1 Tbsp.
¼ cup	6	1¾ tsp.	¼ cup
⅓ cup	8	2½ tsp.	⅓ cup
½ cup	12	3½ tsp.	½ cup
¾ cup	18	5½ tsp	¾ cup
1 cup	24	7¼ tsp.	1 cup
1 lb.	57	5 Tbsp.+2 tsp.**	2¼ cups

*(rounded measurement for easy use)
**equivalent to 1 pouch

Although we've eliminated added table sugar and used as little fat as possible, not all of the recipes in this book qualify as "reduced fat" or "reduced calorie" recipes. The percent calorie reduction from a similar traditional recipe is noted at the bottom of each recipe.

*Although we cannot guarantee the success of recipes not tested in our kitchens, we can offer suggestions for using Equal. Our product works very well in fruit pie fillings, cheesecakes, puddings, toppings and preserves. But keep in mind that cakes, cookies and pastries depend on sugar for bulk, tenderness and browning—properties that no sugar substitute can provide. And, Equal may lose sweetness in some prolonged heating applications. Whenever possible, as in stove-top cooking, simply add the sweetener after the recipe has been removed from the heat.

EQUAL.

Strawberry Smoothie

1 carton (8 ounces) plain nonfat yogurt
¼ cup skim milk
1 teaspoon Equal® Measure™ or 3 packets Equal®
    sweetener or 2 tablespoons Equal® Spoonful™
3 cups frozen strawberries
1 cup ice cubes

● Combine yogurt, milk and Equal® in blender container. With blender running, add berries, a few at a time, through opening in lid. Blend until smooth; add ice cubes one at a time through opening in lid, blending until slushy. Pour into glasses.

Makes 4 (6-ounce) servings

Nutrition information per serving:
Calories: 82, Protein: 4 g, Carbohydrates: 17 g, Fat: 0 g, Cholesterol: 1 mg, Sodium: 58 mg
Food Exchanges: ½ Milk, 1 Fruit

25% calorie reduction from traditional recipe

Left to right: Strawberry Smoothie and Orange Jubilees (page 10)

Orange Jubilee

1 small can (6 ounces) frozen orange juice concentrate
2¼ cups skim milk
½ teaspoon vanilla
1¾ teaspoons Equal® Measure™ or 6 packets Equal®
sweetener or ¼ cup Equal® Spoonful™
8 ice cubes
Ground nutmeg or cinnamon (optional)

● Process orange juice concentrate, milk, vanilla and Equal® in food processor or blender until smooth; add ice cubes and process again until smooth. Serve in small glasses; sprinkle with nutmeg or cinnamon, if desired.

Makes 6 (4-ounce) servings

Nutrition information per serving:
Calories: 94, Protein: 4 g, Carbohydrates: 19 g, Fat: 0 g, Cholesterol: 2 mg, Sodium: 49 mg
Food Exchanges: ½ Milk, 1 Fruit

36% calorie reduction from traditional recipe

Fitness Shake

2 cups skim milk
2 medium-size ripe bananas, cut into 1-inch pieces
½ cup plain or banana nonfat yogurt
½ cup nonfat dry milk powder
⅓ cup wheat germ
1 teaspoon vanilla
2½ teaspoons Equal® Measure™ or 8 packets Equal®
sweetener or ⅓ cup Equal® Spoonful™
Ground cinnamon (optional)

● Blend all ingredients except cinnamon in blender or food processor until smooth. Pour into glasses and sprinkle with cinnamon, if desired. *Makes 4 (8-ounce) servings*

Nutrition information per serving:
Calories: 190, Protein: 12 g, Carbohydrates: 33 g, Fat: 2 g, Cholesterol: 4 mg, Sodium: 134 mg
Food Exchanges: 1½ Milk, 1 Fruit, ½ Fat

42% calorie reduction from traditional recipe

Holiday Eggnog

2 cups skim milk
2 tablespoons cornstarch
3½ teaspoons Equal® Measure™ or 12 packets Equal®
    sweetener or ½ cup Equal® Spoonful™
2 eggs, beaten
2 teaspoons vanilla
¼ teaspoon ground cinnamon
2 cups skim milk, chilled
⅛ teaspoon ground nutmeg

● Mix 2 cups milk, cornstarch and Equal® in small saucepan; heat to boiling. Boil 1 minute, stirring constantly. Mix about half of milk mixture into eggs; return egg mixture to remaining milk in saucepan. Cook over low heat until slightly thickened, stirring constantly. Remove from heat; stir in vanilla and cinnamon. Cool to room temperature; refrigerate until chilled. Stir 2 cups chilled milk into custard mixture; serve in small glasses. Sprinkle with nutmeg. *Makes 8 (4-ounce) servings*

Variation: Stir 1 to 1½ teaspoons rum or brandy extract into eggnog, if desired.

Nutrition information per serving:
Calories: 79, Protein: 6 g, Carbohydrates: 10 g, Fat: 1 g, Cholesterol: 55 mg, Sodium: 79 mg
Food Exchanges: 1 Milk

49% calorie reduction from traditional recipe

Russian-Style Tea

1 tub (0.55 ounces) sugar-free lemonade-flavored soft
    drink mix
1 tub (0.55 ounces) sugar-free orange-flavored breakfast
    beverage crystals
1 cup unsweetened iced tea mix
10½ teaspoons Equal® Measure™ or 36 packets Equal®
    sweetener or 1½ cups Equal® Spoonful™
1 teaspoon ground cinnamon
½ teaspoon *each* ground cloves and ground allspice
    Boiling water

continued on page 12

Russian-Style Tea, continued

● Mix dry ingredients together, stirring well. Measure 1 tablespoon mixture (if prepared with Equal® Measure™ or packets) or 2 tablespoons mixture (if prepared with Equal® Spoonful™) into each 8-ounce mug; fill with boiling water and stir to blend.

● Store remaining mixture in covered jar.

Makes 20 (8-ounce) servings

Nutrition information per serving:
Calories: 18, Protein: 0 g, Carbohydrates: 4 g, Fat: 0 g, Cholesterol: 0 mg, Sodium: 16 mg
Food Exchanges: Free Food

90% calorie reduction from traditional recipe

Coffee Latte

1¼ cups regular grind espresso or other dark roast coffee
1 cinnamon stick, broken into pieces
6 cups water
2½ teaspoons Equal® Measure™ or 8 packets Equal® sweetener or ⅓ cup Equal® Spoonful™
2½ cups skim milk
Ground cinnamon or nutmeg

● Place espresso and cinnamon stick in filter basket of drip coffee pot; brew coffee with water. Stir Equal® into coffee; pour into 8 mugs or cups.

● Heat milk in small saucepan until steaming. Process half of milk in blender at high speed until foamy, about 15 seconds; pour milk into 4 mugs of coffee, spooning foam on top. Repeat with remaining milk and coffee. Sprinkle with cinnamon or nutmeg before serving.   *Makes about 8 (8-ounce) servings*

Nutrition information per serving:
Calories: 31, Protein: 3 g, Carbohydrates: 5 g, Fat: 0 g, Cholesterol: 1 mg, Sodium: 46 mg
Food Exchanges: ½ Milk

61% calorie reduction from traditional recipe

Coffee Lattes

Peach Preserves

2½ to 3 pounds ripe peaches (10 to 12)
2 tablespoons lemon juice
1 package (1¾ ounces) no-sugar-needed pectin
7¼ teaspoons Equal® Measure™ or 24 packets Equal® sweetener or 1 cup Equal® Spoonful™

● Peel, pit and finely chop peaches; measure 4 cups into saucepan. Stir in lemon juice and pectin. Let stand 10 minutes, stirring frequently. Cook and stir until boiling. Cook and stir 1 minute more. Remove from heat; stir in Equal®. Skim off foam.

● Immediately ladle into freezer containers or jars, leaving ½-inch headspace. Seal and label containers. Let stand at room temperature several hours or until set. Store up to 2 weeks in refrigerator or 6 months in freezer.   *Makes 8 (½-pint) jars*

Nutrition information per serving (1 tablespoon):
Calories: 10, Protein: 0 g, Carbohydrates: 3 g, Fat: 0 g, Cholesterol: 0 mg, Sodium: 3 mg
Food Exchanges: Free Food

78% calorie reduction from traditional recipe

Mocha Sauce

1 cup skim milk
4 teaspoons unsweetened cocoa
2 teaspoons cornstarch
1 teaspoon instant coffee crystals
1 teaspoon vanilla
1¼ teaspoons Equal® Measure™ or 4 packets Equal® sweetener or 3 tablespoons Equal® Spoonful™

● Combine milk, cocoa, cornstarch and coffee crystals in small saucepan. Cook and stir until thickened and bubbly. Cook and stir 2 minutes more. Remove from heat; stir in vanilla and Equal®. Cool. Cover and chill.   *Makes about 1 cup*

Nutrition information per serving (1 tablespoon):
Calories: 10, Protein: 1 g, Carbohydrates: 2 g, Fat: 0 g, Cholesterol: 0 mg, Sodium: 8 mg
Food Exchanges: Free Food

73% calorie reduction from traditional recipe

Fresh Cranberry Relish

1 orange
1 package (12 ounces) fresh or thawed frozen cranberries
2 medium tart apples, unpeeled, cored and coarsely chopped
5¼ teaspoons Equal® Measure™ or 18 packets Equal® sweetener or ¾ cup Equal® Spoonful™
⅛ teaspoon salt

● Grate rind from orange and reserve. Peel orange; cut orange into large pieces.

● Place orange rind, orange pieces, cranberries and apples in food processor; process until finely chopped. Stir in Equal® and salt. Refrigerate until ready to serve. *Makes 12 servings*

Note: Amount of Equal® may vary depending on the tartness of the apples and cranberries.

Nutrition information per serving of Fresh Cranberry Relish (⅔ cup):
Calories: 41, Protein: 0 g, Carbohydrates: 10 g, Fat: 0 g, Cholesterol: 0 mg, Sodium: 22 mg
Food Exchanges: ½ Fruit

51% calorie reduction from traditional recipe

Cranberry Gelatin Salad
Prepare 2 packages (0.3 ounces each) sugar-free raspberry gelatin according to package directions using 1½ cups boiling water and 1½ cups cold water; refrigerate until mixture is consistency of unbeaten egg whites. Prepare Fresh Cranberry Relish as directed above; stir into gelatin mixture and spoon into lightly greased 8-cup mold or casserole. Refrigerate until set, about 4 hours. To unmold, briefly dip mold into warm water and loosen top edge of mold with tip of sharp knife. Unmold onto serving plate lined with salad greens. Makes 12 (⅔-cup) servings.

Nutrition information per serving of Cranberry Gelatin Salad (⅔ cup):
Calories: 46, Protein: 1 g, Carbohydrates: 11 g, Fat: 0 g, Cholesterol: 0 mg, Sodium: 60 mg
Food Exchanges: 1 Fruit

66% calorie reduction from traditional recipe

Spiced Fruit Butter

3 pounds apples, pears or peaches
¾ cup apple juice, pear nectar or peach nectar
1 to 2 teaspoons ground cinnamon
½ teaspoon ground nutmeg
⅛ teaspoon ground cloves
5 teaspoons Equal® Measure™ or 16 packets Equal® sweetener or ⅔ cup Equal® Spoonful™

● Peel and core or pit fruit; slice. Combine prepared fruit, fruit juice and spices in Dutch oven. Bring to boiling; cover and simmer until very tender, about 15 minutes. Cool slightly. Purée in batches in blender or food processor. Return to Dutch oven.

● Simmer, uncovered, over low heat until desired consistency, stirring frequently. (This may take up to 1 hour.) Remove from heat; stir in Equal®. Transfer to freezer containers or jars, leaving ½-inch headspace. Store up to 2 weeks in refrigerator or up to 3 months in freezer.   *Makes 6 (½-pint) jars*

Nutrition information per serving (1 tablespoon):
Calories: 16, Protein: 0 g, Carbohydrates: 4 g, Fat: 0 g, Cholesterol: 0 mg, Sodium: 0 mg
Food Exchanges: Free Food

48% calorie reduction from traditional recipe

Strawberry Jam

2 quarts fresh or thawed frozen strawberries
1 package (1¾ ounces) no-sugar-needed pectin
4 tablespoons Equal® Measure™ or 40 packets Equal® sweetener or 1⅔ cup Equal® Spoonful™

● Mash strawberries to make 4 cups pulp. Combine strawberries and pectin in large saucepan. Let stand 10 minutes, stirring frequently. Cook and stir over medium heat until mixture comes to a boil. Cook and stir 1 minute more. Remove from heat; stir in Equal®. Skim off foam if necessary.

continued on page 18

*Left to right: Strawberry Jam
and Spiced Fruit Butter*

Strawberry Jam, continued

● Immediately fill containers, leaving ½-inch headspace. Seal and let stand at room temperature several hours or until set. Store up to 2 weeks in refrigerator or 6 months in freezer.

Makes 4 (½-pint) jars

Nutrition information per serving (1 tablespoon):
Calories: 8, Protein: 0 g, Carbohydrates: 2 g, Fat: 0 g, Cholesterol: 0 mg, Sodium: 0 mg
Food Exchanges: Free Food

83% calorie reduction from traditional recipe

Cranberry Sauce

⅔ **cup water**
 2 cups fresh or frozen cranberries (8 ounces)
7¼ **teaspoons Equal® Measure™ or 24 packets Equal®**
    sweetener or 1 cup Equal® Spoonful™

● Combine water and cranberries in medium saucepan. Bring just to boiling; reduce heat. Boil gently, uncovered, over medium heat 8 minutes, stirring occasionally. (Skins will pop.)

● Remove from heat; mash slightly. Stir in Equal®. Cover and chill. Serve chilled with beef, pork, ham or poultry.

Makes 1½ cups

Orange-Cranberry Sauce
Reduce water to ⅓ cup and add ⅓ cup orange juice. Add 1 teaspoon finely grated orange peel and one orange, peeled, sectioned and chopped, when adding Equal®. Makes 1⅔ cups.

Nutrition information per serving of Cranberry Sauce (2 tablespoons):
Calories: 17, Protein: 0 g, Carbohydrates: 4 g, Fat: 0 g, Cholesterol: 0 mg, Sodium: 0 mg
Food Exchanges: Free Food

76% calorie reduction from traditional recipe

Maple-Flavored Syrup

1 cup apple juice
2½ teaspoons cornstarch
1 tablespoon margarine
1¾ teaspoons Equal® Measure™ or 6 packets Equal®
sweetener or ¼ cup Equal® Spoonful™
1 teaspoon maple flavoring
1 teaspoon vanilla

● Combine apple juice and cornstarch in small saucepan. Cook and stir until thickened and bubbly. Cook and stir 2 minutes more. Remove from heat. Stir in margarine, Equal®, maple flavoring and vanilla. Serve over pancakes, waffles or French toast.   *Makes 1 cup*

Nutrition information per serving (1 tablespoon):
Calories: 18, Protein: 0 g, Carbohydrates: 3 g, Fat: 1 g, Cholesterol: 0 mg, Sodium: 9 mg
Food Exchanges: Free Food

72% calorie reduction from traditional recipe

Raspberry Sauce

2 cups fresh raspberries or thawed frozen unsweetened
raspberries
1 tablespoon orange juice
1¼ teaspoons Equal® Measure™ or 4 packets Equal®
sweetener or 3 tablespoons Equal® Spoonful™
½ teaspoon finely grated orange peel

● Place raspberries in blender container; blend until smooth. Strain through sieve; discard seeds. Stir orange juice, Equal® and orange peel into puréed berries. Serve over fresh fruit, frozen yogurt or cheesecake.   *Makes 1 cup*

Nutrition information per serving (¼ cup):
Calories: 35, Protein: 1 g, Carbohydrates: 9 g, Fat: 0 g, Cholesterol: 0 mg, Sodium: 0 mg
Food Exchanges: ½ Fruit

45% calorie reduction from traditional recipe

Quick Refrigerator Sweet Pickles

5 cups thinly sliced cucumbers
2 cloves garlic, halved
2 cups water
1 teaspoon mustard seed
1 teaspoon celery seed
1 teaspoon ground turmeric
2 cups sliced onions
1 cup julienne carrot strips
2 cups vinegar
**3 tablespoons plus 1¾ teaspoons Equal® Measure™ or
    36 packets Equal® sweetener or 1½ cups Equal®
    Spoonful™**

● Place cucumbers and garlic in glass bowl. Combine water, mustard seed, celery seed and turmeric in medium saucepan. Bring to boiling. Add onions and carrots; cook 2 minutes. Add vinegar; bring just to boiling. Remove from heat; stir in Equal®. Pour over cucumbers and garlic. Cool. Cover and chill at least 24 hours before serving. Store in refrigerator up to 2 weeks.

Makes about 6 cups

Nutrition information per serving (¼ cup):
Calories: 8, Protein: 0 g, Carbohydrates: 3 g, Fat: 0 g, Cholesterol: 0 mg, Sodium: 3 mg
Food Exchanges: Free Food

87% calorie reduction from traditional recipe

Sassy Sweet and Sour Dressing

1 cup plain low-fat yogurt
⅓ cup cider vinegar
2 tablespoons finely chopped onion
**1¾ teaspoons Equal® Measure™ or 6 packets Equal®
    sweetener or ¼ cup Equal® Spoonful™**
1 teaspoon dry mustard
1 teaspoon celery seed
½ teaspoon salt

● Process all ingredients in food processor or blender until smooth and well mixed. Refrigerate until ready to serve.

Makes 12 servings

Variation: Substitute 1 tablespoon poppy seed for celery seed.

Nutrition information per serving (about 2 tablespoons):
Calories: 19, Protein: 1 g, Carbohydrates: 3 g, Fat: 0 g, Cholesterol: 1 mg,
Sodium: 104 mg
Food Exchanges: Free Food

41% calorie reduction from traditional recipe

Triple-Berry Jam

4 cups fresh strawberries or thawed frozen unsweetened strawberries
2 cups fresh raspberries or thawed frozen unsweetened raspberries
1 cup fresh blueberries or thawed frozen unsweetened blueberries
1 package (1¾ ounces) no-sugar-needed pectin
2 tablespoons Equal® Measure™ or 20 packets Equal® sweetener or ¾ cup plus 4 teaspoons Equal® Spoonful™

● Mash strawberries, raspberries and blueberries, by hand or with food processor, to make 4 cups pulp. Stir in pectin; let mixture stand 10 minutes, stirring frequently. Transfer to large saucepan. Cook and stir over medium heat until mixture comes to a boil. Cook and stir 1 minute more. Remove from heat; stir in Equal®. Skim off foam, if necessary.

● Immediately fill containers, leaving ½-inch headspace. Seal and let stand at room temperature until firm (several hours). Store up to 2 weeks in refrigerator or 6 months in freezer.

Makes 8 (½-pint) jars

Nutrition information per serving (1 tablespoon):
Calories: 9, Protein: 0 g, Carbohydrates: 2 g, Fat: 0 g, Cholesterol: 0 mg,
Sodium: 3 mg
Food Exchanges: Free Food

80% calorie reduction from traditional recipe

EQUAL®

Down Home Barbecued Beef

 1 slice bacon
½ cup chopped onion
½ cup ketchup
½ cup apple juice
 1 tablespoon white vinegar
 1 teaspoon prepared mustard
 1 teaspoon Worcestershire sauce
⅛ teaspoon salt
⅛ teaspoon ground black pepper
2½ teaspoons Equal® Measure™ or 8 packets Equal®
     sweetener or ⅓ cup Equal® Spoonful™
 12 ounces thinly sliced roast beef
 4 kaiser rolls (optional)

● Cut bacon into 1-inch pieces; cook in medium saucepan over medium-high heat 3 to 4 minutes or until almost cooked. Add onion; cook 3 to 5 minutes or until bacon is crisp and onion is tender, stirring occasionally.

● Combine ketchup, juice, vinegar, mustard, Worcestershire sauce, salt and pepper; add to bacon mixture. Reduce heat; cover and simmer until flavors are blended, 15 to 20 minutes.

● Stir in Equal® and sliced beef. Serve warm on rolls, if desired.

Makes 4 servings

continued on page 24

Down Home Barbecued Beef

Down Home Barbecued Beef, continued

Microwave Directions
Cut bacon into 1-inch pieces and place in 1½-quart microwavable casserole. Cook, uncovered, at HIGH 1 minute. Add onion and cook at HIGH for 2½ to 3 minutes or until bacon is crisp and onion is tender, stirring once. Combine ketchup, apple juice, vinegar, mustard, Worcestershire sauce, salt and pepper; add to bacon mixture. Cook, covered, at HIGH 4 to 5 minutes or until boiling. Cook at MEDIUM 8 to 10 minutes or until flavors are blended, stirring twice. Stir in Equal® and sliced beef. Serve warm.

Nutrition information per serving:
Calories: 223, Protein: 26 g, Carbohydrates: 16 g, Fat: 6 g,
Cholesterol: 70 mg, Sodium: 542 mg
Food Exchanges: 3 Meat, 1 Bread

23% calorie reduction from traditional recipe

Shredded Carrot and Raisin Salad

　1 **pound carrots, peeled and shredded**
1½ **cups thinly sliced, cored, peeled apples**
　¼ **cup dark raisins**
　½ **cup plain low-fat yogurt or sour cream**
　⅓ **cup skim milk**
　1 **tablespoon lemon juice**
1½ **teaspoons Equal® Measure or 5 packets Equal®**
　　　sweetener or 3½ tablespoons Equal® Spoonful™
　¼ **teaspoon ground nutmeg**
　¼ **teaspoon ground cinnamon**

● Combine carrots, apples and raisins in large bowl. Combine remaining ingredients; spoon over carrot mixture and toss to coat. Refrigerate until chilled.　　*Makes 6 servings*

Nutrition information per serving:
Calories: 90, Protein: 3 g, Carbohydrates: 20 g, Fat: 0 g, Cholesterol: 1 mg,
Sodium: 48 mg
Food Exchanges: 1 Vegetable, 1 Fruit

37% calorie reduction from traditional recipe

Oriental-Style Sea Scallops

2 tablespoons sesame or vegetable oil
1½ cups broccoli flowerets
1 cup thinly sliced onion
1 pound sea scallops
3 cups thinly sliced napa cabbage or bok choy
2 cups snow peas, ends trimmed
1 cup shiitake or button mushrooms, sliced
2 cloves garlic, minced
2 teaspoons ground star anise*
¼ teaspoon ground coriander*
½ cup chicken broth
¼ cup rice wine vinegar
2 to 3 teaspoons reduced-sodium soy sauce
¼ cup cold water
2 tablespoons cornstarch
1 to 1½ teaspoons Equal® Measure™ or 3 to 4 packets
    Equal® sweetener or 2 to 3 tablespoons
    Equal® Spoonful™
4 cups hot cooked rice

● Heat oil in wok or large skillet. Stir-fry broccoli and onion
3 to 4 minutes. Add scallops, cabbage, snow peas, mushrooms,
garlic, anise and coriander; stir-fry 2 to 3 minutes.

● Add chicken broth, vinegar and soy sauce; heat to boiling.
Reduce heat and simmer, uncovered, until scallops are cooked
and vegetables are tender, about 5 minutes. Heat to boiling.

● Mix cold water and cornstarch. Stir cornstarch mixture into
boiling mixture; boil, stirring constantly, until thickened. Remove
from heat; let stand 2 to 3 minutes. Stir in Equal® Serve over
rice.   *Makes 6 servings*

*Or, substitute 2 teaspoons five-spice powder for star anise and
coriander; amounts of vinegar and soy sauce may need to be adjusted
to taste.

***Nutrition information per serving (2 ounces scallops and
⅔ cup rice):***
*Calories: 330, Protein: 20 g, Carbohydrates: 49 g, Fat: 6 g,
Cholesterol: 26 mg, Sodium: 276 mg
Food Exchanges: 2 Meat, 2½ Bread, 1 Vegetable*

20% calorie reduction from traditional recipe

Oriental Garden Toss

⅓ cup thinly sliced green onions
3 tablespoons reduced-sodium soy sauce
3 tablespoons water
1½ teaspoons roasted sesame oil
1 teaspoon Equal® Measure™ or 3 packets Equal®
    sweetener or 2 tablespoons Equal® Spoonful™
¼ teaspoon garlic powder
⅛ teaspoon crushed red pepper flakes
1 package (3 ounces) low-fat ramen noodle soup
2 cups fresh pea pods, halved crosswise
1 cup fresh bean sprouts
1 cup sliced fresh mushrooms
1 can (8¾ ounces) baby corn, drained and halved
    crosswise
1 red bell pepper, cut into bite-size strips
3 cups shredded Chinese cabbage
⅓ cup chopped lightly salted cashews (optional)

● Combine green onions, soy sauce, water, sesame oil, Equal®, garlic powder and red pepper flakes in screw-top jar; set aside.

● Break up ramen noodles (discard seasoning packet); combine with pea pods in large bowl. Pour boiling water over mixture to cover. Let stand 1 minute; drain.

● Combine noodles, pea pods, bean sprouts, mushrooms, baby corn and bell pepper in large bowl. Shake dressing and add to noodle mixture; toss to coat. Cover and chill 2 to 24 hours. Just before serving, add shredded cabbage; toss to combine. Sprinkle with cashews, if desired.   *Makes 6 (1-cup) servings*

Nutrition information per serving:
Calories: 124, Protein: 6 g, Carbohydrates: 21 g, Fat: 2 g, Cholesterol: 0 mg, Sodium: 605 mg
Food Exchanges: 1 Vegetable, 1 Bread, ½ Fat

31% calorie reduction from traditional recipe

Oriental Garden Toss

Penne Salad with Spring Peas

**1 pound penne or medium pasta shells, cooked and
cooled**
1½ cups fresh or thawed frozen peas, cooked
1 large yellow or red bell pepper, sliced
½ cup sliced green onions and tops
1 cup skim milk
½ cup fat-free mayonnaise
½ cup red wine vinegar
¼ cup minced parsley
**2 teaspoons drained green peppercorns, crushed
(optional)**
**1¾ teaspoons Equal® Measure™ or 6 packets Equal®
sweetener or ¼ cup Equal® Spoonful™**
Salt and pepper

● Combine pasta, peas, bell pepper and green onions in salad
bowl. Blend milk and mayonnaise in medium bowl until smooth.
Stir in vinegar, parsley, peppercorns and Equal®.

● Pour dressing over salad and toss to coat; season to taste
with salt and pepper.   *Makes 6 (1-cup) servings*

Nutrition information per serving:
*Calories: 190, Protein: 8 g, Carbohydrates: 36 g, Fat: 1 g,
Cholesterol: 26 mg, Sodium: 188 mg
Food Exchanges: 2 Bread*

63% calorie reduction from traditional recipe

Penne Salad with Spring Peas

Cabbage Slaw

1 small head cabbage (1 pound), thinly sliced
½ cup chopped green bell pepper
½ cup chopped onion
2 tablespoons chopped pimiento or red bell pepper
½ cup cider vinegar
3 tablespoons vegetable oil
2½ teaspoons Equal® Measure™ or 8 packets Equal®
    sweetener or ⅓ cup Equal® Spoonful™
1 teaspoon celery seed
½ teaspoon dry mustard
¼ teaspoon salt
⅛ teaspoon ground black pepper

● Combine cabbage, green pepper, onion and pimiento in medium bowl.

● Measure remaining ingredients into jar; cover with lid and shake to blend well. Pour dressing over cabbage mixture and toss to coat. Refrigerate until ready to serve.

Makes 12 (½-cup) servings

Nutrition information per serving:
Calories: 49, Protein: 1 g, Carbohydrates: 4 g, Fat: 4 g, Cholesterol: 0 mg, Sodium: 52 mg
Food Exchanges: 1 Vegetable, ½ Fat

37% calorie reduction from traditional recipe

Triple Bean Salad

1 can (14½ ounces) green beans, drained
1 can (14½ ounces) wax beans, drained
1 can (15½ ounces) dark kidney beans, drained
¼ cup sliced green onions
¼ cup red wine vinegar
1 tablespoon olive oil
1 teaspoon Equal® Measure™ or 3 packets Equal®
    sweetener or 2 tablespoons Equal® Spoonful™
1 teaspoon dried basil leaves
1 small clove garlic, minced
¼ teaspoon salt
¼ teaspoon fresh ground pepper

● Combine green beans, wax beans, kidney beans, green onions, vinegar, oil, Equal®, basil, garlic, salt and pepper in large nonmetallic bowl. Mix well. Cover; refrigerate overnight. Serve chilled.   *Makes 4 (1-cup) servings*

Nutrition information per serving:
Calories: 174, Protein: 8 g, Carbohydrates: 29 g, Fat: 4 g, Cholesterol: 0 mg, Sodium: 1025 mg
Food Exchanges: 1½ Bread, 1 Vegetable, ½ Fat

39% calorie reduction from traditional recipe

Grandma's Noodle Kugel

¼ **cup margarine, softened**
 3 **eggs**
1½ **cups reduced-fat cottage cheese**
 1 **cup reduced-fat sour cream**
 1 **can (20 ounces) crushed pineapple in juice, drained**
 ½ **cup dark raisins**
5½ **teaspoons Equal® Measure™ or 18 packets Equal® sweetener or ¾ cup Equal® Spoonful™**
 ½ **teaspoon ground cinnamon**
 1 **package (12 ounces) cholesterol-free wide noodles, cooked**

● Mix margarine and eggs in large bowl until smooth; blend in cottage cheese, sour cream, pineapple, raisins, Equal® and cinnamon. Mix in noodles.

● Spoon mixture evenly into lightly greased 13×9×2-inch baking dish. Bake kugel, uncovered, in preheated 325°F oven until heated through, 45 to 55 minutes. Cut into squares.
                    Makes 12 servings

Nutrition information per serving:
Calories: 261, Protein: 10 g, Carbohydrates: 31 g, Fat: 8 g, Cholesterol: 62 mg, Sodium: 200 mg
Food Exchanges: 1 Milk, ½ Fruit, 1 Bread, 1½ Fat

22% calorie reduction from traditional recipe

Fresh Greens with Hot Bacon Dressing

3 cups torn spinach leaves
3 cups torn romaine lettuce
2 small tomatoes, cut into wedges
1 cup sliced mushrooms
1 medium carrot, shredded
1 slice bacon, cut into small pieces
3 tablespoons red wine vinegar
1 tablespoon water
¼ teaspoon dried tarragon, crushed
⅛ teaspoon coarsely ground pepper
¼ teaspoon Equal® Measure™ or 1 packet Equal®
**   sweetener or 2 teaspoons Equal® Spoonful™**

● Combine spinach, romaine, tomatoes, mushrooms and carrot in large bowl; set aside.

● Cook bacon in 12-inch skillet until crisp. Carefully stir in vinegar, water, tarragon and pepper. Heat to boiling; remove from heat. Stir in Equal®.

● Add spinach mixture to skillet. Toss 30 to 60 seconds or just until greens are wilted. Transfer to serving bowl. Serve immediately.   *Makes 4 to 6 (1⅓-cup) servings*

Nutrition information per serving:
Calories: 51, Protein: 3 g, Carbohydrates: 9 g, Fat: 1 g, Cholesterol: 1 mg, Sodium: 74 mg
Food Exchanges: 1½ Vegetable

43% calorie reduction from traditional recipe

*Fresh Greens with
Hot Bacon Dressing*

Sweet and Sour Stir-Fry

1 tablespoon vegetable oil
1 pound boneless skinless chicken breasts, cut into
   3-inch strips
1 can (8 ounces) sliced water chestnuts, drained
1 cup 2×½-inch red bell pepper strips
¼ cup chopped onion
2 tablespoons cornstarch
2 tablespoons soy sauce
1 tablespoon white vinegar
1 can (8 ounces) pineapple chunks, packed in juice,
   undrained
¼ teaspoon ground ginger
¼ teaspoon salt
1¾ teaspoons Equal® Measure™ or 6 packets Equal®
   sweetener or ¼ cup Equal® Spoonful™
1 package (6 ounces) frozen pea pods

● Heat oil in wok or skillet. Add chicken; cook until chicken is no longer pink, 5 to 6 minutes. Remove and set aside. Add water chestnuts, pepper and onion to wok; cook until vegetables are tender, 3 to 4 minutes, stirring constantly.

● Combine cornstarch, soy sauce and vinegar in small bowl; stir to dissolve cornstarch. Add pineapple with juice, ginger and salt. Add to vegetable mixture; cook until sauce thickens, 2 to 3 minutes, stirring constantly.

● Stir in Equal®. Add pea pods and chicken; cook until pea pods and chicken are heated through, 2 to 3 minutes.

Makes 4 servings

Nutrition information per serving:
Calories: 272, Protein: 29 g, Carbohydrates: 27 g, Fat: 5 g,
Cholesterol: 66 mg, Sodium: 620 mg
Food Exchanges: 1 Bread, 3 Meat, 2 Vegetable

21% calorie reduction from traditional recipe

Sweet and Sour Stir-Fry

Grilled Fish with Pineapple-Cilantro Sauce

1 medium pineapple (about 2 pounds), peeled, cored and
    cut into scant 1-inch chunks
¾ cup unsweetened pineapple juice
2 tablespoons lime juice
2 cloves garlic, minced
½ to 1 teaspoon minced jalapeño pepper
2 tablespoons minced cilantro
2 tablespoons cold water
1 tablespoon cornstarch
1 to 1½ teaspoons Equal® Measure™ or 3 to 4 packets
    Equal® sweetener or 2 to 3 tablespoons Equal®
    Spoonful™
Salt and pepper
6 halibut, haddock or salmon steaks or fillets (about
    4 ounces each), grilled

● Heat pineapple, pineapple juice, lime juice, garlic and jalapeño pepper to boiling in medium saucepan. Reduce heat and simmer, uncovered, 5 minutes. Stir in cilantro; heat to boiling.

● Mix cold water and cornstarch; stir into boiling mixture. Boil, stirring constantly, until thickened. Remove from heat; cool 2 to 3 minutes.

● Stir in Equal®; season to taste with salt and pepper. Serve warm sauce over fish.   *Makes 6 servings*

Note: Pineapple-Cilantro Sauce is also excellent served with pork or lamb.

Nutrition information per serving:
Calories: 185, Protein: 24 g, Carbohydrates: 16 g, Fat: 3 g,
Cholesterol: 36 mg, Sodium: 159 mg
Food Exchanges: 2½ Meat, 1 Fruit

26% calorie reduction from traditional recipe

All-American Barbecued Beans

1 slice bacon
½ cup chopped onion
½ cup ketchup
2 tablespoons white vinegar
2 tablespoons water
1 teaspoon prepared mustard
1 teaspoon Worcestershire sauce
⅛ teaspoon salt
⅛ teaspoon ground black pepper
1 can (15½ ounces) Great Northern beans, drained
2½ teaspoons Equal® Measure™ or 8 packets Equal®
    sweetener or ⅓ cup Equal® Spoonful™

● Cut bacon into 1-inch pieces; cook in medium saucepan over medium-high heat 3 to 4 minutes. Add onion and cook until bacon is crisp and onion is tender, stirring occasionally.

● Combine ketchup, vinegar, water, mustard, Worcestershire sauce, salt and pepper; add to bacon mixture. Stir in beans. Reduce heat and simmer, covered, until flavors are blended, 15 to 20 minutes. Stir in Equal®.   *Makes 4 (½-cup) servings*

Microwave Directions
Cut bacon into 1-inch pieces and place in 1½-quart microwavable casserole. Cook uncovered at HIGH 1 minute. Add onion and cook at HIGH 2½ to 3 minutes, stirring once. Combine ketchup, vinegar, water, mustard, Worcestershire sauce, salt and pepper; add to bacon mixture. Stir in beans and cover with lid or plastic wrap. Cover and cook at HIGH 4 minutes, then cook at MEDIUM 8 to 10 minutes or until flavors are blended, stirring twice. Stir in Equal®.

Nutrition information per serving:
Calories: 185, Protein: 9 g, Carbohydrates: 36 g, Fat: 1 g, Cholesterol: 1 mg, Sodium: 491 mg
Food Exchanges: 2 Bread, 1 Vegetable

25% calorie reduction from traditional recipe

Chicken and Fruit Salad

½ cup plain nonfat yogurt
½ to 1 teaspoon lemon-pepper seasoning
½ teaspoon dry mustard
¼ teaspoon garlic salt
¼ teaspoon poppy seed
1¼ teaspoons Equal® Measure™ or 4 packets Equal®
    sweetener or 3 tablespoons Equal® Spoonful™
1 to 2 tablespoons orange juice
4 cups torn spinach leaves
8 ounces thinly sliced cooked chicken breast
2 cups sliced strawberries
1 cup halved seedless green grapes
1½ cups thinly sliced yellow summer squash
2 medium oranges, peeled and sectioned
½ cup toasted pecan pieces (optional)

● Combine yogurt, lemon-pepper seasoning, mustard, garlic salt, poppy seed and Equal® in small bowl. Add enough orange juice to reach drizzling consistency; set aside.

● Line platter with spinach. Arrange chicken, strawberries, grapes, squash and orange sections over spinach. Drizzle salad with dressing. Sprinkle with pecans, if desired.

Makes 4 servings

Nutrition information per serving:
Calories: 202, Protein: 21 g, Carbohydrates: 20 g, Fat: 5 g,
Cholesterol: 51 mg, Sodium: 380 mg
Food Exchanges: ½ Vegetable, 1 Fruit, 2½ Meat

45% calorie reduction from traditional recipe

Chicken and Fruit Salad

EQUAL®

Pies & Tarts

Chocolate Cream Pie

Reduced-Fat Pie Pastry (page 59) or favorite pastry for
  9-inch pie
⅓ cup cornstarch
¼ to ⅓ cup European or Dutch-process cocoa
10¾ teaspoons Equal® Measure™ or 36 packets Equal®
  sweetener or 1½ cups Equal® Spoonful™
⅛ teaspoon salt
3 cups skim milk
2 eggs
2 egg whites
1 teaspoon vanilla
8 tablespoons thawed frozen light whipped topping
  Chocolate leaves (optional)

● Roll pastry on lightly floured surface into circle 1 inch larger than inverted 9-inch pie pan. Ease pastry into pan; trim and flute edge. Pierce bottom and side of pastry with fork. Bake in preheated 425°F oven until crust is browned, 10 to 15 minutes. Cool on wire rack.

● Combine cornstarch, cocoa, Equal® and salt in medium saucepan; stir in milk. Heat to boiling over medium-high heat, whisking constantly. Boil until thickened, about 1 minute.

● Beat eggs and egg whites in small bowl; whisk about 1 cup chocolate mixture into eggs. Whisk egg mixture into chocolate mixture in saucepan. Cook over very low heat, whisking constantly, 30 to 60 seconds. Remove from heat; stir in vanilla.

continued on page 42

Chocolate Cream Pie

Chocolate Cream Pie, continued

● Spread hot filling in baked crust; refrigerate until chilled and set, about 6 hours. Cut into wedges and place on serving plates; garnish each serving with dollop of whipped topping and chocolate leaves, if desired. *Makes 8 servings*

Nutrition information per serving:
Calories: 234, Protein: 8 g, Carbohydrates: 32 g, Fat: 8 g,
Cholesterol: 55 mg, Sodium: 245 mg
Food Exchanges: ½ Milk, 1½ Bread, 1½ Fat

43% calorie reduction from traditional recipe

Nectarine and Berry Pie

Reduced-Fat Pie Pastry (page 59) or favorite pastry for 9-inch pie
5 cups sliced nectarines (about 5 medium)
1 cup raspberries or sliced strawberries
1 cup fresh or frozen blueberries, partially thawed
2 teaspoons lemon juice
3 tablespoons cornstarch
7¼ teaspoons Equal® Measure™ or 24 packets Equal® sweetener or 1 cup Equal® Spoonful™
1 teaspoon grated lemon peel
¼ teaspoon ground allspice

● Roll pastry on floured surface into 12-inch circle; transfer to ungreased cookie sheet.

● Toss nectarines and berries with lemon juice in large bowl; sprinkle fruit with combined cornstarch, Equal®, lemon peel and allspice and toss to coat. Arrange fruit over pastry, leaving 2-inch border around edge of pastry. Bring edge of pastry toward center, overlapping as necessary. Bake pie in preheated 425°F oven until pastry is golden and fruit is tender, 35 to 40 minutes. Cool on wire rack. *Makes 8 servings*

Nutrition information per serving:
Calories: 216, Protein: 3 g, Carbohydrates: 38 g, Fat: 7 g, Cholesterol: 0 mg,
Sodium: 138 mg
Food Exchanges: 1½ Fruit, 1 Bread, 1½ Fat

39% calorie reduction from traditional recipe

Rhubarb-Strawberry Pie

Reduced-Fat Pie Pastry (page 59) or favorite pastry for 9-inch pie
3 cups 1-inch rhubarb pieces or 1 package (16 ounces) frozen unsweetened rhubarb, thawed, undrained
¾ cup water
¼ cup all-purpose flour
3 tablespoons cornstarch
2 tablespoons lemon juice
3 cups sliced strawberries
12¼ teaspoons Equal® Measure™ or 40 packets Equal® sweetener or 1⅔ cups Equal® Spoonful™
¼ teaspoon ground nutmeg

● Roll pastry on lightly floured surface into circle 1 inch larger than inverted 9-inch pie pan. Ease pastry into pan; trim and flute edge. Pierce bottom and side of pastry with fork. Bake in preheated 425°F oven until pastry is browned, 10 to 15 minutes. Cool on wire rack.

● Cook rhubarb in large covered saucepan over medium heat until rhubarb releases liquid, about 5 minutes. Combine water, flour, cornstarch and lemon juice; stir into rhubarb and heat to boiling. Reduce heat and simmer, uncovered, until mixture is thickened and rhubarb is almost tender, 3 to 5 minutes, stirring frequently. Stir in strawberries and cook 2 to 3 minutes longer.

● Stir Equal® and nutmeg into fruit mixture; spoon into baked crust, spreading evenly. Bake in 350°F oven until bubbly, about 40 minutes. Cover edge of crust with aluminum foil if browning too quickly. Cool briefly on wire rack; serve warm.

Makes 8 servings

Nutrition information per serving:
Calories: 199, Protein: 3 g, Carbohydrates: 33 g, Fat: 6 g, Cholesterol: 0 mg, Sodium: 138 mg
Food Exchanges: 1 Bread, 1 Fruit, 1 Fat

41% calorie reduction from traditional recipe

Cherry Lattice Pie

2 packages (16 ounces each) frozen no-sugar-added pitted cherries
12¾ teaspoons Equal® Measure™ or 42 packets Equal® sweetener or 1¾ cup Equal® Spoonful™
4 teaspoons all-purpose flour
4 teaspoons cornstarch
¼ teaspoon ground nutmeg
5 to 7 drops red food color
Reduced-Fat Pie Pastry (page 59, 2 recipes for double crust) or favorite pastry for double-crust 9-inch pie

● Thaw cherries completely in strainer set in bowl; reserve ¾ cup cherry juice. Mix Equal®, flour, cornstarch and nutmeg in small saucepan; stir in cherry juice and heat to boiling. Boil, stirring constantly, 1 minute. Remove from heat and stir in cherries; stir in food color.

● Roll half of pastry on floured surface into circle 1 inch larger than inverted 9-inch pie pan; ease pastry into pan. Pour cherry mixture into pastry. Roll remaining pastry on floured surface to ⅛-inch thickness; cut into 10 to 12 strips, ½ inch wide. Arrange pastry strips over filling and weave into lattice design. Trim ends of lattice strips; fold edge of lower crust over ends of lattice strips. Seal and flute edge.

● Bake in preheated 425°F oven until pastry is browned, 35 to 40 minutes. Cool on wire rack.   *Makes 8 servings*

Nutrition information per serving:
Calories: 330, Protein: 5 g, Carbohydrates: 51 g, Fat: 12 g, Cholesterol: 0 mg, Sodium: 269 mg
Food Exchanges: 1½ Fruit, 2 Bread, 2½ Fat

46% calorie reduction from traditional recipe

Cherry Lattice Pie

Key Lime Pie

1 cup graham cracker crumbs
3 tablespoons melted margarine
1 teaspoon Equal® Measure™ or 3 packets Equal®
  sweetener or 2 tablespoons Equal® Spoonful™
1 envelope (¼ ounce) unflavored gelatin
1¾ cups skim milk
  1 package (8 ounces) reduced-fat cream cheese, softened
⅓ to ½ cup fresh lime juice
3½ teaspoons Equal® Measure™ or 12 packets Equal®
  sweetener or ½ cup Equal® Spoonful™
  Lime slices, raspberries and fresh mint sprigs, for
  garnish (optional)

● Combine graham cracker crumbs, margarine and 1 teaspoon Equal® Measure™ *or* 3 packets Equal® sweetener *or* 2 tablespoons Equal® Spoonful™ in bottom of 7-inch springform pan; pat evenly on bottom and ½ inch up side of pan.

● Sprinkle gelatin over ½ cup milk in small saucepan; let stand 2 to 3 minutes. Cook over low heat, stirring constantly, until gelatin is dissolved. Beat cream cheese in small bowl until fluffy; beat in remaining 1¼ cups milk and gelatin mixture. Mix in lime juice and 3½ teaspoons Equal® Measure™ *or* 12 packets Equal® sweetener *or* ½ cup Equal® Spoonful™. Refrigerate pie until set, about 2 hours.

● To serve, loosen side of pie from pan with small spatula and remove side of pan. Place pie on serving plate; garnish with lime slices, raspberries and mint, if desired.

Makes 8 servings

Nutrition information per serving:
Calories: 150, Protein: 6 g, Carbohydrates: 11 g, Fat: 10 g,
Cholesterol: 16 mg, Sodium: 231 mg
Food exchanges: 1 Bread, 2 Fat

46% calorie reduction from traditional recipe

Key Lime Pie

Banana Cream Pie

**Reduced-Fat Pie Pastry (page 59) or favorite pastry for
  9-inch pie**
⅓ **cup cornstarch**
3½ **teaspoons Equal® Measure™ or 12 packets Equal®
  sweetener or ½ cup Equal® Spoonful™**
⅛ **teaspoon salt**
2½ **cups skim milk**
 2 **egg yolks**
 1 **teaspoon vanilla**
 2 **bananas, sliced**
 3 **egg whites**
¼ **teaspoon cream of tartar**
3½ **teaspoons Equal® Measure™ or 12 packets Equal®
  sweetener***

*Equal® Spoonful™ cannot be used in meringue recipes.

● Roll pastry on lightly floured surface into circle 1 inch larger
than inverted 9-inch pie pan. Ease pastry into pan; trim and flute
edge. Pierce bottom and side of pastry with fork. Bake in
preheated 425°F oven until crust is browned, 10 to 15 minutes.
Cool on wire rack.

● Combine cornstarch, 3½ teaspoons Equal® Measure™ *or*
12 packets Equal® sweetener *or* ½ cup Equal® Spoonful™ and
salt in medium saucepan; stir in milk. Heat to boiling over
medium-high heat, whisking constantly. Boil until thickened,
about 1 minute, whisking constantly.

● Beat egg yolks and vanilla in small bowl; whisk about 1 cup
hot custard mixture into eggs. Whisk egg mixture back into
custard mixture in saucepan. Cook over very low heat, whisking
constantly, 30 to 60 seconds. Arrange bananas in bottom of
baked crust; pour custard mixture over bananas, spreading
evenly.

● Beat egg whites in medium bowl with electric mixer until
foamy; add cream of tartar and beat to soft peaks. Gradually
beat in 3½ teaspoons Equal® Measure™ *or* 12 packets Equal®
sweetener, beating until stiff peaks form. Spread meringue over
hot custard mixture, carefully sealing to edge of crust. Bake in
preheated 425°F oven until meringue is browned, about

2 minutes. Cool on wire rack 30 minutes; refrigerate until set and chilled, about 6 hours. Cut just before serving.

Makes 8 servings

Nutrition information per serving:
Calories: 230, Protein: 7 g, Carbohydrates: 34 g, Fat: 7 g,
Cholesterol: 55 mg, Sodium: 230 mg
Food Exchanges: ½ Milk, 2 Bread, 1½ Fat

33% calorie reduction from traditional recipe

Sweet Potato Pie

Reduced-Fat Pie Pastry (page 59) or favorite pastry for 9-inch pie
2 cups mashed cooked sweet potatoes (about 2 pounds)
1 can (12 ounces) evaporated skim milk
2 eggs, lightly beaten
7¼ teaspoons Equal® Measure™ or 24 packets Equal® sweetener or 1 cup Equal® Spoonful™
1 tablespoon margarine, softened
1 tablespoon all-purpose flour
1½ teaspoons vanilla
1½ to 2 teaspoons ground cinnamon
¾ teaspoon ground nutmeg
¼ teaspoon ground mace (optional)
½ teaspoon salt

● Roll pastry on floured surface into circle 1 inch larger than inverted 9-inch pie pan. Ease into pan; trim and flute edge. Blend remaining ingredients in large bowl until smooth. Pour into pastry shell.

● Bake in preheated 425°F oven 20 minutes; reduce heat to 350°F and bake until filling is set and sharp knife inserted near center comes out clean, 30 to 35 minutes. Cool completely on wire rack; refrigerate until serving time.

Makes 8 servings

Nutrition information per serving:
Calories: 264, Protein: 8 g, Carbohydrates: 37 g, Fat: 9 g,
Cholesterol: 55 mg, Sodium: 361 mg
Food Exchanges: 1 Vegetable, 2 Bread, 2 Fat

41% calorie reduction from traditional recipe

Spiced Pumpkin Pie

Reduced-Fat Pie Pastry (page 59) or favorite pastry for
   9-inch pie
1 can (16 ounces) pumpkin
1 can (12 ounces) evaporated skim milk
3 eggs
5½ teaspoons Equal® Measure™ or 18 packets Equal®
   sweetener or ¾ cup Equal® Spoonful™
¼ teaspoon salt
1 teaspoon ground cinnamon
½ teaspoon ground ginger
¼ teaspoon ground nutmeg
⅛ teaspoon ground cloves

● Roll pastry on floured surface into circle 1 inch larger than inverted 9-inch pie pan. Ease into pan; trim and flute edge.

● Beat pumpkin, evaporated milk and eggs in medium bowl; beat in remaining ingredients. Pour into pastry shell. Bake in preheated 425°F oven 15 minutes; reduce heat to 350°F and bake until knife inserted near center comes out clean, about 40 minutes. Cool on wire rack.   *Makes 8 servings*

Nutrition information per serving:
*Calories: 219, Protein: 9 g, Carbohydrates: 28 g, Fat: 8 g,
Cholesterol: 81 mg, Sodium: 282 mg
Food Exchanges: 2 Bread, 1½ Fat*

41% calorie reduction from traditional recipe

Country Peach Tart

Reduced-Fat Pie Pastry (page 59) or favorite pastry for
   9-inch pie
1 tablespoon all-purpose flour
2½ teaspoons Equal® Measure™ or 8 packets Equal®
   sweetener or ⅓ cup Equal® Spoonful™
4 cups sliced, pitted, peeled fresh peaches (about
   4 medium) or frozen peaches, thawed
Ground nutmeg

continued on page 52

Spiced Pumpkin Pie

Country Peach Tart, continued

● Roll pastry on floured surface into 12-inch circle; transfer to ungreased cookie sheet. Combine flour and Equal®; sprinkle over peaches. Toss to coat. Arrange peaches over pastry, leaving 2-inch border around edge. Sprinkle lightly with nutmeg. Bring pastry edge toward center, overlapping as necessary. Bake tart in preheated 425°F oven until crust is browned and fruit is tender, 25 to 30 minutes.   *Makes 8 servings*

Nutrition information per serving:
Calories: 168, Protein: 3 g, Carbohydrates: 27 g, Fat: 6 g, Cholesterol: 0 mg, Sodium: 134 mg
Food Exchanges: ½ Fruit, 1½ Bread, 1 Fat

34% calorie reduction from traditional recipe

Apple-Raisin Sour Cream Pie

1½ cups graham cracker crumbs
⅓ cup margarine, melted
1¾ teaspoons Equal® Measure™ or 6 packets Equal® sweetener or ¼ cup Equal® Spoonful™
4 cups sliced, cored, peeled Granny Smith or other baking apples (4 to 6 medium)
2 teaspoons lemon juice
¼ cup dark raisins
½ cup reduced-fat sour cream
1 egg white, beaten
3½ teaspoons Equal® Measure™ or 12 packets Equal® sweetener or ½ cup Equal® Spoonful™
1 tablespoon all-purpose flour
¼ teaspoon ground cinnamon
⅛ teaspoon ground nutmeg

● Mix graham cracker crumbs, margarine, and 1¾ teaspoons Equal® Measure™ *or* 6 packets Equal® sweetener *or* ¼ cup Equal® Spoonful™ in bottom of 9-inch springform pan. Reserve ¼ cup mixture; press remaining mixture firmly on bottom and 1 inch up side of pan. Bake in preheated 350°F oven until lightly browned, 5 to 8 minutes. Cool on wire rack.

● Toss apples with lemon juice in large bowl; add raisins. Combine sour cream and remaining ingredients; spoon mixture over apples, mixing until apples are coated.

Spoon apple mixture into crust; sprinkle with reserved ¼ cup crumb mixture.

● Bake pie in 350°F oven until apples are tender, about 55 minutes. Cool on wire rack. Remove side of pan; place pie on serving plate.   *Makes 8 servings*

Nutrition information per serving:
Calories: 245, Protein: 3 g, Carbohydrates: 33 g, Fat: 12 g,
Cholesterol: 6 mg, Sodium: 239 mg
Food Exchanges: 1 Bread, 1 Fruit, 2½ Fat

25% calorie reduction from traditional recipe

Coconut Custard Pie

Reduced-Fat Pie Pastry (page 59) or favorite pastry for 9-inch pie
4 eggs
¼ teaspoon salt
2 cups skim milk
5½ teaspoons Equal® Measure™ or 18 packets Equal® sweetener or ¾ cup Equal® Spoonful™
2 teaspoons coconut extract
½ cup flaked coconut

● Roll pastry on floured surface into circle 1 inch larger than inverted 9-inch pie pan. Ease into pan; trim and flute edge.

● Beat eggs and salt in large bowl until thick and lemon colored, about 5 minutes. Mix in milk and remaining ingredients. Pour mixture into pastry shell.

● Bake pie in preheated 425°F oven 15 minutes. Reduce temperature to 350°F and bake until sharp knife inserted halfway between center and edge of pie comes out clean, 20 to 25 minutes. Cool on wire rack. Serve at room temperature, or refrigerate and serve chilled.
                                    Makes 8 servings

Nutrition information per serving:
Calories: 213, Protein: 7 g, Carbohydrates: 23 g, Fat: 10 g,
Cholesterol: 107 mg, Sodium: 275 mg
Food Exchanges: 1 Milk, ½ Bread, 2 Fat

40% calorie reduction from traditional recipe

Mile-High Apple Pie

Reduced-Fat Pie Pastry (page 59, 2 recipes for double crust) or favorite pastry for double crust 9-inch pie
3 tablespoons cornstarch
7¼ teaspoons Equal® Measure™ or 24 packets Equal® sweetener or 1 cup Equal® Spoonful™
¾ teaspoon ground cinnamon
¼ teaspoon ground nutmeg
¼ teaspoon salt
8 cups sliced, cored, peeled Granny Smith or other baking apples (about 8 medium)

● Roll half the pastry on floured surface into circle 1 inch larger than inverted 9-inch pie pan. Ease pastry into pan.

● Combine cornstarch, Equal®, cinnamon, nutmeg and salt; sprinkle over apples in large bowl and toss. Arrange apple mixture in pie crust.

● Roll remaining pastry into circle large enough to fit top of pie. Cut out hearts from pastry with cookie cutters. Place remaining pastry on pie; seal edges, trim and flute. Press heart cut-outs on pastry. Bake in preheated 425°F oven until pastry is golden and apples are tender, 40 to 50 minutes. Cool on wire rack.

Makes 8 servings

Nutrition information per serving:
Calories: 334, Protein: 4 g, Carbohydrates: 53 g, Fat: 12 g,
Cholesterol: 0 mg, Sodium: 335 mg
Food Exchanges: 1 Fruit, 2½ Bread, 2½ Fat

39% calorie reduction from traditional recipe

Mile-High Apple Pie

Mom's Lemon Meringue Pie

**Reduced-Fat Pie Pastry (page 59) or favorite pastry for
9-inch pie
2¼ cups water
½ cup lemon juice
10¾ teaspoons Equal® Measure™ or 36 packets Equal®
sweetener or 1½ cups Equal® Spoonful™
⅓ cup plus 2 tablespoons cornstarch
2 eggs
2 egg whites
1 teaspoon finely grated lemon peel (optional)
2 tablespoons margarine
1 to 2 drops yellow food color (optional)
3 egg whites
¼ teaspoon cream of tartar
3½ teaspoons Equal® Measure™ or 12 packets Equal®
sweetener***

*Equal® Spoonful™ cannot be used in meringue recipes.

● Roll pastry on lightly floured surface into circle 1 inch larger
than inverted 9-inch pie pan. Ease pastry into pan; trim and flute
edge. Pierce bottom and side of pastry with fork. Bake in
preheated 425°F oven until pastry is browned, 10 to 15 minutes.
Cool on wire rack.

● Mix water, lemon juice, 10¾ teaspoons Equal® Measure™ *or*
36 packets Equal® sweetener *or* 1½ cups Equal® Spoonful™ and
cornstarch in medium saucepan. Heat to boiling over medium-
high heat, stirring constantly; boil and stir 1 minute. Beat eggs
and 2 egg whites in small bowl; stir in about half of hot
cornstarch mixture. Stir egg mixture back into remaining
cornstarch mixture in saucepan; cook and stir over low heat
1 minute. Remove from heat; add margarine, stirring until
melted. Stir in food color, if desired. Pour mixture into baked pie
shell.

● Beat 3 egg whites in medium bowl with electric mixer until
foamy; add cream of tartar and beat to soft peaks. Gradually
beat in 3½ teaspoons Equal® Measure™ *or* 12 packets Equal®

continued on page 58

Mom's Lemon Meringue Pie

Mom's Lemon Meringue Pie, continued

sweetener, beating until stiff peaks form. Spread meringue over hot lemon filling, carefully sealing to edge of crust to prevent shrinking or weeping.

● Bake pie in preheated 425°F oven until meringue is browned, about 5 minutes. Cool completely on wire rack before cutting.

Makes 8 servings

Nutrition information per serving:
Calories: 233, Protein: 6 g, Carbohydrates: 29 g, Fat: 10 g, Cholesterol: 53 mg, Sodium: 223 mg
Food Exchanges: 2 Bread, 2 Fat

50% calorie reduction from traditional recipe

Blueberry Lattice Pie

6 cups fresh blueberries or 2 packages (16 ounces each) frozen unsweetened blueberries
3 tablespoons lemon juice
6 tablespoons cornstarch
8 teaspoons Equal® Measure™ or 27 packets Equal® sweetener or 1 cup plus 2 tablespoons Equal® Spoonful™
Reduced-Fat Pie Pastry (page 59, 2 recipes for double crust) or favorite pastry for double crust 9-inch pie

● Toss blueberries and lemon juice in large bowl. Sprinkle with combined cornstarch and Equal® and toss to coat. Let stand 30 minutes.

● Roll half of pastry on lightly floured surface into circle 1 inch larger than inverted 9-inch pie pan. Ease pastry into pan; trim within 1 inch of edge of pan. Roll remaining pastry to ⅛-inch thickness; cut into 10 to 12 strips, ½ inch wide.

● Pour blueberry mixture into pastry. Arrange pastry strips over filling and weave into lattice design. Trim ends of lattice strips; fold edge of lower crust over ends of lattice strips. Seal and flute edge.

● Bake in preheated 425°F oven until crust is browned and filling is bubbly, about 1 hour. Cover edge of crust with aluminum foil if browning too quickly. Cool on wire rack; refrigerate leftovers. *Makes 8 servings*

Nutrition information per serving:
Calories: 345, Protein: 5 g, Carbohydrates: 55 g, Fat: 12 g, Cholesterol: 0 mg, Sodium: 143 mg
Food Exchanges: 2 Bread, 1½ Fruit, 2½ Fat

41% calorie reduction from traditional recipe

Reduced-Fat Pie Pastry

1¼ cups all-purpose flour
1 teaspoon Equal® Measure™ or 3 packets Equal® sweetener or 2 tablespoons Equal® Spoonful™
¼ teaspoon salt
4 tablespoons cold margarine, cut into pieces
5 to 5½ tablespoons ice water

● Combine flour, Equal® and salt in medium bowl; cut in margarine with pastry blender until mixture resembles coarse crumbs. Mix in water, 1 tablespoon at a time, stirring lightly with fork after each addition until dough is formed. Wrap and refrigerate until ready to use.

● For prebaked crust, roll pastry on lightly floured surface into circle 1 inch larger than inverted 9-inch pie pan. Ease pastry into pan; trim and flute edge. Pierce bottom and side of pastry with fork. Bake in preheated 425°F oven until pastry is browned, 10 to 15 minutes. Cool on wire rack.
Makes pastry for 9-inch pie (8 servings)

Tip: Double recipe for double crust or lattice pies.

Nutrition information per serving:
Calories: 123, Protein: 2 g, Carbohydrates: 15 g, Fat: 6 g, Cholesterol: 0 mg, Sodium: 134 mg
Food Exchanges: 1 Bread, 1 Fat

50% reduction in fat compared to traditional recipe

Summer Fruit Tart

1¼ **cups all-purpose flour**
¼ **teaspoon salt**
⅓ **cup shortening**
3 **to 4 tablespoons cold water**
¼ **cup plain nonfat yogurt**
¼ **cup reduced-fat dairy sour cream**
½ **teaspoon Equal® Measure™ or 2 packets Equal®**
    sweetener or 4 teaspoons Equal® Spoonful™
¼ **teaspoon almond extract**
4 **cups assorted fresh fruit**
¾ **cup pineapple juice**
1 **tablespoon lemon juice**
2 **teaspoons cornstarch**
1 **teaspoon Equal® Measure™ or 3 packets Equal®**
    sweetener or 2 tablespoons Equal® Spoonful™

● Combine flour and salt; cut in shortening. Sprinkle water over mixture; toss with fork until moistened. Form into a ball.

● Roll pastry on lightly floured surface into 10- or 11-inch circle and place in 9- or 10-inch tart pan with removable bottom. Press pastry up side; trim excess. Prick with fork. Line with foil. Bake in preheated 450°F oven 8 minutes. Remove foil; bake until golden, 5 to 6 minutes. Cool on wire rack.

● Combine yogurt, sour cream, ½ teaspoon Equal® Measure™ *or* 2 packets Equal® sweetener *or* 4 teaspoons Equal® Spoonful™ and almond extract. Spread over cooled crust. Arrange fruit on top.

● Combine pineapple juice, lemon juice and cornstarch in small saucepan. Cook and stir until thickened and bubbly. Cook and stir 2 minutes more. Remove from heat; stir in 1 teaspoon Equal® Measure™ *or* 3 packets Equal® sweetener *or* 2 tablespoons Equal® Spoonful™. Cool. Spoon over fruit; cover and chill.   *Makes 10 servings*

Nutrition information per serving:
Calories: 166, Protein: 3 g, Carbohydrates: 22 g, Fat: 8 g, Cholesterol: 1 mg, Sodium: 65 mg
Food Exchanges: ½ Fruit, 1 Bread, 1½ Fat

20% calorie reduction from traditional recipe

Summer Fruit Tart

EQUAL®

Cakes, Cookies & Breads

Rich Chocolate Cheesecake

1¼ cups graham cracker crumbs
 4 tablespoons margarine, melted
 1 teaspoon Equal® Measure™ or 3 packets Equal®
    sweetener™ or 2 tablespoons Equal® Spoonful™
 2 packages (8 ounces each) reduced-fat cream cheese,
    softened
 1 package (8 ounces) fat-free cream cheese, softened
5½ teaspoons Equal® Measure™ or 18 packets Equal®
    sweetener or ¾ cup Equal® Spoonful™
 2 eggs
 2 egg whites
 2 tablespoons cornstarch
 1 cup reduced-fat sour cream
 ⅓ cup European or Dutch-process cocoa
 1 teaspoon vanilla
    Fresh mint sprigs, raspberries, nonfat whipped topping
    and orange peel (optional)

● Mix graham cracker crumbs, margarine and 1 teaspoon
Equal® Measure™ *or* 3 packets Equal® sweetener *or*
2 tablespoons Equal® Spoonful™ in bottom of 9-inch springform
pan. Pat mixture evenly on bottom and ½ inch up side of pan.

● Beat cream cheese and 5½ teaspoons Equal® Measure™ *or*
18 packets Equal® sweetener *or* ¾ cup Equal® Spoonful™ in
large bowl until fluffy; beat in eggs, egg whites and cornstarch.
Mix in sour cream, cocoa and vanilla until well blended. Pour
mixture into crust.

continued on page 64

Rich Chocolate Cheesecake

● Place cheesecake in roasting pan on oven rack; add 1 inch hot water to roasting pan. Bake cheesecake in preheated 300°F oven just until set in the center, 45 to 50 minutes. Remove cheesecake from roasting pan; return cheesecake to oven. Turn oven off and let cheesecake cool 3 hours in oven with door ajar. Refrigerate 8 hours or overnight. Remove side of pan; place cheesecake on serving plate. Garnish, if desired.

Makes 16 servings

Nutrition information per serving:
Calories: 189, Protein: 8 g, Carbohydrates: 14 g, Fat: 11 g, Cholesterol: 51 mg, Sodium: 280 mg
Food Exchanges: 1 Milk, 2 Fat

39% calorie reduction from traditional recipe

Granola Bites

2 cups cornflakes cereal
⅔ cup quick-cooking oats
¼ cup 100% bran cereal
½ cup chopped pitted dates or raisins
½ cup reduced-fat crunchy peanut butter
4 egg whites or ½ cup real liquid egg product
5 teaspoons Equal® Measure™ or 16 packets Equal® sweetener or ⅔ cup Equal® Spoonful™
2 teaspoons vanilla

● Combine cornflakes, oats, bran cereal and dates in large bowl. Mix peanut butter, egg whites, Equal® and vanilla in small bowl until smooth; pour over cereal mixture and stir until all ingredients are coated.

● Shape mixture into 1-inch mounds; place on lightly greased cookie sheets. Bake in preheated 350°F oven until cookies are set and browned, 8 to 10 minutes. Cool on wire racks.

Makes about 2 dozen cookies

Nutrition information per serving (1 cookie):
Calories: 67, Protein: 3 g, Carbohydrates: 9 g, Fat: 3 g, Cholesterol: 0 mg, Sodium: 61 mg
Food Exchanges: ½ Bread, ½ Fat

36% calorie reduction from traditional recipe

Orange Chiffon Cheesecake

2 cups graham cracker crumbs
8 tablespoons light margarine, melted
1 teaspoon Equal® Measure™ or 3 packets Equal®
   sweetener or 2 tablespoons Equal® Spoonful™
1 cup orange juice
1 envelope (¼ ounce) unflavored gelatin
12 ounces reduced-fat cream cheese, softened
1 cup part-skim ricotta cheese
3½ teaspoons Equal® Measure™ or 12 packets Equal®
   sweetener or ½ cup Equal® Spoonful™
2 cups light whipped topping
2 medium oranges, peeled, seeded and chopped
   Orange sections (optional)

● Spray 9-inch springform pan with nonstick cooking spray. Mix graham cracker crumbs, margarine and 1 teaspoon Equal® Measure™ *or* 3 packets Equal® sweetener *or* 2 tablespoons Equal® Spoonful™. Pat mixture evenly on bottom and halfway up side of pan. Bake in preheated 350°F oven 8 to 10 minutes or until set. Cool.

● Pour orange juice into small saucepan. Sprinkle gelatin over orange juice and let soften 1 minute. Heat, stirring constantly, until gelatin dissolves, about 3 minutes. Blend cream cheese and ricotta cheese in large bowl until smooth; stir in 3½ teaspoons Equal® Measure™ *or* 12 packets Equal® sweetener *or* ½ cup Equal® Spoonful™. Add gelatin mixture to cheese mixture; blend until smooth. Fold whipped topping into cheese mixture. Stir in chopped oranges. Spoon into prepared crust and spread evenly.

● Chill 6 hours or overnight. Remove side of pan; place cheesecake on serving plate. Garnish with orange sections, if desired.   *Makes 16 servings*

Nutrition information per serving:
*Calories: 204, Protein: 6 g, Carbohydrates: 20 g, Fat: 11 g,
Cholesterol: 17 mg, Sodium: 209 mg
Food Exchanges: ½ Milk, 1 Bread, 2 Fat*

29% calorie reduction from traditional recipe

Apricot-Almond Coffee Ring

1 cup dried apricots, sliced
1 cup water
3½ teaspoons Equal® Measure™ or 12 packets Equal®
    sweetener or ½ cup Equal® Spoonful™
⅛ teaspoon ground mace
1 loaf (16 ounces) frozen Italian bread dough, thawed
⅓ cup sliced or slivered almonds
    Skim milk
1 teaspoon Equal® Measure™ or 3 packets Equal®
    sweetener or 2 tablespoons Equal® Spoonful™

● Heat apricots, water, 3½ teaspoons Equal® Measure™ *or* 12 packets Equal® sweetener *or* ½ cup Equal® Spoonful™ and mace to boiling in small saucepan; reduce heat and simmer, covered, until apricots are tender and water is absorbed, about 10 minutes. Simmer, uncovered, until no water remains, 2 to 3 minutes. Cool.

● Roll dough on floured surface into 14×8-inch rectangle. Spread apricot mixture on dough to within 1 inch of edges; sprinkle with ¼ cup almonds. Roll dough up jelly-roll style, beginning with long edge; pinch edge of dough to seal. Place dough seam side down on greased cookie sheet, forming circle; pinch ends to seal.

● Using scissors, cut dough from outside edge almost to center, making cuts 1 inch apart. Turn each section cut side up so filling shows. Let rise, covered, in warm place until dough is double in size, about 1 hour.

● Brush top of dough lightly with milk; sprinkle with remaining almonds and 1 teaspoon Equal® Measure™ *or* 3 packets Equal® sweetener *or* 2 tablespoons Equal® Spoonful™. Bake coffee cake in preheated 375°F oven until golden, 25 to 30 minutes. Cool on wire rack.   *Makes about 12 servings*

Nutrition information per serving:
Calories: 154, Protein: 4 g, Carbohydrates: 27 g, Fat: 3 g, Cholesterol: 0 mg, Sodium: 180 mg
Food Exchanges: ½ Fruit, 1 Bread, ½ Fat

19% calorie reduction from traditional recipe

Apricot-Almond Coffee Ring

Pineapple Upside-Down Cake

1 can (14 ounces) unsweetened crushed pineapple in
   juice, undrained
¼ cup pecan pieces (optional)
2 tablespoons lemon juice
1¾ teaspoons Equal® Measure™ or 6 packets Equal®
   sweetener or ¼ cup Equal® Spoonful™
1 teaspoon cornstarch
4 tablespoons margarine, at room temperature
3½ teaspoons Equal® Measure™ or 12 packets Equal®
   sweetener or ½ cup Equal® Spoonful™
1 egg
1 cup cake flour
1½ teaspoons baking powder
½ teaspoon baking soda
¼ teaspoon ground cinnamon
¼ teaspoon ground nutmeg
⅛ teaspoon ground ginger
⅓ cup buttermilk

● Drain pineapple, reserving ¼ cup juice. Mix pineapple,
pecans, 1 tablespoon lemon juice, 1¾ teaspoons Equal®
Measure™ or 6 packets Equal® sweetener or ¼ cup Equal®
Spoonful™ and cornstarch in bottom of 8-inch square or 9-inch
round cake pan; spread mixture evenly in pan.

● Beat margarine and 3½ teaspoons Equal® Measure™ or
12 packets Equal® sweetener or ½ cup Equal® Spoonful™ in
medium bowl until fluffy; beat in egg. Combine flour, baking
powder, baking soda and spices in small bowl. Add to margarine
mixture alternately with buttermilk, ¼ cup reserved pineapple
juice and remaining 1 tablespoon lemon juice, beginning and
ending with dry ingredients. Spread batter over pineapple
mixture in cake pan.

● Bake in preheated 350°F oven until browned and toothpick
inserted in center comes out clean, about 25 minutes. Invert
cake immediately onto serving plate. Serve warm or at room
temperature.   *Makes 8 servings*

continued on page 70

Pineapple Upside-Down Cake

Pineapple Upside-Down Cake, continued

Note: If desired, maraschino cherry halves may be placed in bottom of cake pan with pineapple mixture.

Nutrition information per serving:
Calories: 156, Protein: 3 g, Carbohydrates: 22 g, Fat: 7 g,
Cholesterol: 27 mg, Sodium: 257 mg
Food Exchanges: 1½ Bread, 1 Fat

46% calorie reduction from traditional recipe

New York Cheesecake

1¼ **cups vanilla wafer crumbs**
  4 **tablespoons margarine, melted**
  1 **teaspoon Equal® Measure™ or 3 packets Equal®**
      sweetener or 2 tablespoons Equal® Spoonful™
  2 **packages (8 ounces each) reduced-fat cream cheese,**
      softened
  1 **package (8 ounces) fat-free cream cheese, softened**
5½ **teaspoons Equal® Measure™ or 18 packets Equal®**
      sweetener or ¾ cup Equal® Spoonful™
  2 **eggs**
  2 **egg whites**
  2 **tablespoons cornstarch**
  1 **cup reduced-fat sour cream**
  1 **teaspoon vanilla**
  1 **pint strawberries, sliced (optional)**
      Strawberry Sauce (page 71)

● Mix vanilla wafer crumbs, margarine and 1 teaspoon Equal® Measure™ *or* 3 packets Equal® sweetener *or* 2 tablespoons Equal® Spoonful™ in bottom of 9-inch springform pan. Reserve 1 tablespoon of crumb mixture. Pat remaining mixture evenly on bottom and ½ inch up side of pan. Bake in preheated 350°F oven until crust is lightly browned, about 8 minutes. Cool on wire rack.

● Beat cream cheese and 5½ teaspoons Equal® Measure™ *or* 18 packets Equal® sweetener *or* ¾ cup Equal® Spoonful™ in large bowl until fluffy; beat in eggs, egg whites and cornstarch. Mix in sour cream and vanilla until well blended. Pour mixture into crust.

● Place cheesecake in roasting pan on oven rack; add 1 inch hot water to roasting pan. Bake in preheated 300°F oven just until set in the center, 45 to 60 minutes. Remove cheesecake from roasting pan, sprinkle with reserved crumbs and return to oven. Turn oven off and let cheesecake cool 3 hours in oven with door ajar. Refrigerate 8 hours or overnight.

● Remove side of pan; place cheesecake on serving plate. Serve with strawberries and Strawberry Sauce.

Makes 16 servings

Nutrition information per serving:
*Calories: 187, Protein: 7 g, Carbohydrates: 13 g, Fat: 12 g,
Cholesterol: 56 mg, Sodium: 253 mg
Food Exchanges: 1 Milk, 2½ Fat*

39% calorie reduction from traditional recipe

Strawberry Sauce

**1 package (16 ounces) frozen unsweetened strawberries, thawed
1 tablespoon lemon juice
1¾ teaspoons Equal® Measure™ or 6 packets Equal® sweetener or ¼ cup Equal® Spoonful™**

● Process strawberries in food processor or blender until smooth. Stir in lemon juice and Equal®; refrigerate until serving time.

Makes about 2 cups

Nutrition information per serving (2 tablespoons):
*Calories: 12, Protein: 0 g, Carbohydrates: 3 g, Fat: 0 g, Cholesterol: 0 mg,
Sodium: 1 mg
Food Exchanges: Free Food*

45% calorie reduction from traditional recipe

Blueberry Triangles

1½ cups fresh or frozen blueberries, slightly thawed
3½ teaspoons Equal® Measure™ or 12 packets Equal®
    sweetener or ½ cup Equal® Spoonful™
1½ teaspoons cornstarch
  2 to 4 teaspoons cold water
    Reduced-Fat Pie Pastry (page 59) or favorite pastry for
      9-inch pie
    Skim milk
½ teaspoon Equal® Measure™ or 1½ packets Equal®
    sweetener or 1 tablespoon Equal® Spoonful™

● Rinse blueberries; drain slightly and place in medium saucepan. Sprinkle berries with 3½ teaspoons Equal® Measure™ *or* 12 packets Equal® sweetener *or* ½ cup Equal® Spoonful™ and cornstarch; toss to coat. Cook over medium heat, stirring constantly, until berries begin to release juice and form small amount of thickened sauce. (Add water, 1 teaspoon at a time, if bottom of saucepan becomes dry.) Cool; refrigerate until chilled.

● Roll pastry on floured surface to ⅛-inch thickness; cut into 8 (5-inch) squares, rerolling scraps as necessary. Place scant 2 tablespoons blueberry mixture on each pastry square. Fold squares in half to form triangles and press edges together to seal. Flute edges of pastry or crimp with tines of fork; pierce tops of pastries 3 or 4 times with tip of knife.

● Brush tops of pastries lightly with milk and sprinkle with ½ teaspoon Equal® Measure™ *or* 1½ packets Equal® sweetener *or* 1 tablespoon Equal® Spoonful™. Bake on foil- or parchment-lined cookie sheet in preheated 400°F oven until pastries are browned, about 25 minutes.   *Makes 8 triangles*

Nutrition information per serving (1 triangle):
Calories: 147, Protein: 2 g, Carbohydrates: 21 g, Fat: 6 g, Cholesterol: 0 mg, Sodium: 134 mg
Food Exchanges: ½ Fruit, 1 Bread, 1 Fat

43% calorie reduction from traditional recipe

Blueberry Triangles

Date Cake Squares

1¼ cups water
1 cup chopped dates
¾ cup chopped pitted prunes
½ cup dark raisins
8 tablespoons margarine, cut into pieces
2 eggs
1 teaspoon vanilla
1 cup all-purpose flour
5½ teaspoons Equal® Measure™ or 18 packets Equal®
    sweetener or ¾ cup Equal® Spoonful™
1 teaspoon baking soda
½ teaspoon ground cinnamon
¼ teaspoon ground nutmeg
¼ teaspoon salt
¼ cup chopped walnuts

● Combine water, dates, prunes, and raisins in medium saucepan; heat to boiling. Reduce heat and simmer, uncovered, until fruit is tender and water is absorbed, about 10 minutes. Remove from heat and add margarine, stirring until melted; cool to room temperature.

● Mix eggs and vanilla into fruit mixture; mix in combined flour, Equal®, baking soda, cinnamon, nutmeg and salt. Spread batter evenly in greased 11×7×2-inch baking dish; sprinkle with walnuts.

● Bake in preheated 350°F oven until cake springs back when touched lightly, 30 to 35 minutes. Cool on wire rack; cut into squares.   *Makes 2 dozen squares*

Nutrition information per serving (1 square):
Calories: 117, Protein: 2 g, Carbohydrates: 17 g, Fat: 5 g,
Cholesterol: 18 mg, Sodium: 126 mg
Food Exchanges: ½ Fruit, ½ Bread, 1 Fat

15% calorie reduction from traditional recipe

Date Cake Squares

Cream Cheese and Jelly Cookies

¾ cup margarine, softened
1 package (8 ounces) reduced-fat cream cheese, softened
2½ teaspoons Equal® Measure™ or 8 packets Equal®
    sweetener or ⅓ cup Equal® Spoonful™
2 cups all-purpose flour
¼ teaspoon salt
¼ cup black cherry or seedless raspberry spreadable fruit

● Beat margarine, cream cheese and Equal® in medium bowl until fluffy; mix in flour and salt to form a soft dough. Cover and refrigerate until dough is firm, about 3 hours.

● Roll dough on lightly floured surface into circle ⅛ inch thick; cut into rounds with 3-inch cutter. Place rounded ¼ teaspoon spreadable fruit in center of each round; fold rounds into halves and crimp edges firmly with tines of fork. Pierce tops of cookies with tip of sharp knife. Bake cookies on greased cookie sheets in preheated 350°F oven until lightly browned, about 10 minutes. Cool on wire racks. *Makes about 3 dozen*

Nutrition information per serving (1 cookie):
Calories: 80, Protein: 1 g, Carbohydrates: 7 g, Fat: 5 g, Cholesterol: 4 mg, Sodium: 78 mg
Food Exchanges: ½ Bread, 1 Fat

15% calorie reduction from traditional recipe

Chocolate Cream Cheese Frosting

2 packages (8 ounces each) fat-free cream cheese, at
    room temperature
7¼ teaspoons Equal® Measure™ or 24 packets Equal
    sweetener or 1 cup Equal® Spoonful™
2 to 3 tablespoons skim milk
½ cup European or Dutch-process cocoa
1 teaspoon vanilla

● Beat cream cheese, Equal® and 1 tablespoon milk in small bowl until fluffy. Beat in cocoa, vanilla and enough remaining milk to make spreading consistency.

Makes about 2 cups (enough to frost 2-layer cake)

Nutrition information per serving (about 2½ tablespoons):
Calories: 51, Protein: 6 g, Carbohydrates: 6 g, Fat: 0 g, Cholesterol: 7 mg,
Sodium: 229 mg
Food Exchanges: ½ Milk

77% calorie reduction from traditional recipe

Chewy Coconut Bars

 2 eggs
**7¼ teaspoons Equal® Measure™ or 24 packets Equal®
    sweetener or 1 cup Equal® Spoonful™**
¼ teaspoon maple flavoring
½ cup margarine, melted
 1 teaspoon vanilla
½ cup all-purpose flour
 1 teaspoon baking powder
¼ teaspoon salt
 1 cup unsweetened coconut,* finely chopped
½ cup chopped walnuts (optional)
½ cup raisins

● Beat eggs, Equal® and maple flavoring in medium bowl; mix
in margarine and vanilla. Combine flour, baking powder and
salt in small bowl; stir into egg mixture. Mix in coconut, walnuts
and raisins. Spread batter evenly in greased 8-inch square
baking pan.

● Bake in preheated 350°F oven until browned and toothpick
inserted in center comes out clean, about 20 minutes. Cool in
pan on wire rack; cut into squares.   *Makes 16 bars*

*Unsweetened coconut can be purchased in health food stores. Or,
substitute sweetened coconut and decrease amount of Equal® to 5¼
teaspoons Equal® Measure™ *or* 18 packets Equal® sweetener *or* ¾ cup
Equal® Spoonful™.

Nutrition information per serving (1 bar):
Calories: 126, Protein: 2 g, Carbohydrates: 10 g, Fat: 9 g,
Cholesterol: 27 mg, Sodium: 141 mg
Food Exchanges: ½ Bread, 2 Fat

41% calorie reduction from traditional recipe

Raspberry-Almond Bars

2 cups all-purpose flour
3½ teaspoons Equal® Measure™ or 12 packets Equal®
     sweetener or ½ cup Equal® Spoonful™
⅛ teaspoon salt
8 tablespoons cold margarine, cut into pieces
1 egg
1 tablespoon skim milk or water
2 teaspoons grated lemon peel
⅔ cup seedless raspberry spreadable fruit
1 teaspoon cornstarch
½ cup chopped toasted almonds, walnuts or pecans

● Combine flour, Equal® and salt in medium bowl, cut in
margarine with pastry blender until mixture resembles coarse
crumbs. Mix in egg, milk and lemon peel. (Mixture will be
crumbly.)

● Press mixture evenly into bottom of greased 11×7-inch
baking dish. Bake in preheated 400°F oven until edges of crust
are browned, about 15 minutes. Cool on wire rack.

● Mix spreadable fruit and cornstarch in small saucepan; heat
to boiling. Boil until thickened, stirring constantly, 1 minute; cool
slightly. Spread mixture evenly over cooled crust; sprinkle with
almonds. Bake in 400°F oven until spreadable fruit is thick and
bubbly, about 15 minutes. Cool on wire rack; cut into squares.

Makes 2 dozen bars

Nutrition information per serving (1 bar):
Calories: 116, Protein: 2 g, Carbohydrates: 15 g, Fat: 6 g, Cholesterol: 9 mg,
Sodium: 59 mg
Food Exchanges: 1 Bread, 1 Fat

34% calorie reduction from traditional recipe

Raspberry-Almond Bars

Orange Cream Cheese Glaze

4 ounces reduced-fat cream cheese, softened
½ to 1 teaspoon orange extract
1 teaspoon Equal® Measure™ or 3 packets Equal®
sweetener or 2 tablespoons Equal® Spoonful™
Skim milk

● Mix cream cheese, orange extract, Equal® and enough milk to make medium glaze consistency. *Makes about ½ cup*

Nutrition information per serving (1½ teaspoons):
Calories: 18, Protein: 1 g, Carbohydrates: 1 g, Fat: 1 g, Cholesterol: 4 mg,
Sodium: 22 mg
Food Exchanges: Free Food

33% calorie reduction from traditional recipe

Banana Walnut Bread

½ cup skim milk
2 eggs
4 tablespoons margarine, softened
7¼ teaspoons Equal® Measure™ or 24 packets Equal®
sweetener or 1 cup Equal® Spoonful™
1 teaspoon vanilla
½ teaspoon banana extract
1¼ cups mashed ripe bananas (about 2 large)
1¾ cups all-purpose flour
1 teaspoon baking soda
1 teaspoon ground cinnamon
½ teaspoon salt
¼ teaspoon baking powder
⅓ cup coarsely chopped walnuts

● Beat milk, eggs, margarine, Equal®, vanilla and banana extract in large bowl with electric mixer 30 seconds; add bananas and beat on high speed 1 minute.

● Add combined flour, baking soda, cinnamon, salt and baking powder, mixing just until blended. Stir in walnuts. Spread mixture evenly in greased 8½×4½×2½-inch loaf pan.

● Bake in preheated 350°F oven until bread is golden and toothpick inserted in center comes out clean, about 60 minutes. Cool in pan on wire rack 5 minutes; remove from pan and cool on wire rack. *Makes 1 loaf (about 16 slices)*

Nutrition information per serving (1 slice):
Calories: 127, Protein: 3 g, Carbohydrates: 17 g, Fat: 5 g,
Cholesterol: 27 mg, Sodium: 199 mg
Food Exchanges: 1 Bread, 1 Fat

35% calorie reduction from traditional recipe

Date Bran Muffins

1½ cups 100% bran cereal
1½ cups skim milk
⅓ cup margarine, melted
1 egg
1 teaspoon vanilla
1¼ cups all-purpose flour
4¼ teaspoons Equal® Measure™ or 14 packets Equal®
sweetener or ½ cup plus 4 teaspoons Equal®
Spoonful™
1 tablespoon baking powder
2 teaspoons ground cinnamon
½ teaspoon salt
½ cup pitted dates, chopped

● Combine cereal and milk in medium bowl; let stand 5 minutes. Stir in margarine, egg, and vanilla. Add combined flour, Equal®, baking powder, cinnamon and salt, stirring just until mixture is blended. Stir in dates.

● Spoon batter into greased muffin pans; bake in preheated 375°F oven until muffins are browned and toothpicks inserted in centers come out clean, 20 to 25 minutes. Cool in pans on wire rack 5 minutes; remove from pans and cool on wire rack.
Makes 1 dozen

Nutrition information per serving (1 muffin):
Calories: 164, Protein: 5 g, Carbohydrates: 27 g, Fat: 6 g,
Cholesterol: 18 mg, Sodium: 390 mg
Food Exchanges: 2 Bread, 1 Fat

18% calorie reduction from traditional recipe

Pineapple Zucchini Bread

1 cup vegetable oil
3 eggs
3½ teaspoons Equal® Measure™ or 12 packets Equal®
    sweetener or ½ cup Equal® Spoonful™
1 teaspoon vanilla
2 cups shredded zucchini
1 can (8½ ounces) unsweetened crushed pineapple in
    juice, drained
3 cups all-purpose flour
1½ teaspoons ground cinnamon
1 teaspoon baking soda
¾ teaspoon ground nutmeg
¾ teaspoon salt
1 cup raisins
½ cup chopped walnuts, optional

● Mix oil, eggs, Equal® and vanilla in large bowl; stir in zucchini and pineapple. Combine flour, cinnamon, baking soda, nutmeg and salt in medium bowl; stir into oil mixture. Stir in raisins and walnuts, if desired. Spread batter evenly in 2 greased and floured 8½×4½×2½-inch loaf pans.

● Bake in preheated 350°F oven until breads are golden and toothpick inserted in centers comes out clean, 50 to 60 minutes. Cool in pans on wire rack 10 minutes; remove from pans and cool completely on wire rack.

Makes 2 loaves (about 16 slices each)

Nutrition information per serving (1 slice):
*Calories: 134, Protein: 2 g, Carbohydrates: 14 g, Fat: 7 g,
Cholesterol: 20 mg, Sodium: 97 mg
Food Exchanges: 1 Bread, 1 Fat*

26% calorie reduction from traditional recipe

Pineapple Zucchini Bread

EQUAL.

More Desserts

Fruit Baked Apples

3½ teaspoons Equal® Measure™ or 12 packets Equal®
   sweetener or ½ cup Equal® Spoonful™
1 tablespoon cornstarch
   Pinch ground cinnamon
   Pinch ground nutmeg
2 cups apple cider or juice
1 package (6 ounces) dried mixed fruit, chopped
1 tablespoon margarine
8 tart baking apples

● Combine Equal®, cornstarch, cinnamon and nutmeg in medium saucepan; stir in cider. Add dried fruit; heat to boiling. Reduce heat and simmer, uncovered, until fruit is tender and cider mixture is reduced to about 1 cup, 10 to 15 minutes. Add margarine and stir until melted.

● Remove cores from apples, cutting to but not through bottoms. Peel 1 inch around tops. Place apples in greased baking pan. Fill centers with fruit; spoon remaining cider mixture over apples.

● Bake, uncovered, in preheated 350°F oven until fork-tender, about 45 minutes.   *Makes 8 servings*

Nutrition information per serving:
Calories: 176, Protein: 1 g, Carbohydrates: 42 g, Fat: 2 g, Cholesterol: 0 mg, Sodium: 22 mg
Food Exchanges: 2½ Fruit, ½ Fat

34% calorie reduction from traditional recipe

Fruit Baked Apples

Creamy Tapioca Pudding

2 cups skim milk
3 tablespoons quick-cooking tapioca
1 egg
⅛ teaspoon salt
3½ teaspoons Equal® Measure™ or 12 packets Equal
    sweetener or ½ cup Equal® Spoonful™
1 to 2 teaspoons vanilla
    Ground cinnamon and nutmeg

● Combine milk, tapioca, egg and salt in medium saucepan. Let stand 5 minutes. Cook over medium-high heat, stirring constantly, until boiling. Remove from heat; stir in Equal® and vanilla.

● Spoon mixture into serving dishes; sprinkle lightly with cinnamon and nutmeg. Serve warm, or refrigerate and serve chilled.　　　　　*Makes 4 (⅔-cup) servings*

Nutrition information per serving:
Calories: 101, Protein: 6 g, Carbohydrates: 16 g, Fat: 1 g,
Cholesterol: 55 mg, Sodium: 146 mg
Food Exchanges: 1 Bread, ½ Milk

57% calorie reduction from traditional recipe

Baked Vanilla Custard

1 quart skim milk
6 eggs
6¼ teaspoons Equal® Measure™ or 21 packets Equal®
    sweetener or ¾ cup plus 2 tablespoons
    Equal® Spoonful™
2 teaspoons vanilla
¼ teaspoon salt
    Ground nutmeg

● Heat milk just to boiling in medium saucepan; let cool 5 minutes.

● Beat eggs, Equal®, vanilla and salt in large bowl until smooth; gradually beat in hot milk. Pour mixture into 10 custard cups or 1½-quart glass casserole; sprinkle generously with nutmeg. Place custard cups or casserole in roasting pan; add 1 inch hot water to roasting pan.

● Bake, uncovered, in preheated 325°F oven until sharp knife inserted halfway between center and edge of custard comes out clean, 45 to 60 minutes. Remove custard dishes from roasting pan; cool on wire rack. Refrigerate until chilled.

Makes 10 (½-cup) servings

Nutrition information per serving:

Calories: 90, Protein: 7 g, Carbohydrates: 8 g, Fat: 3 g, Cholesterol: 129 mg, Sodium: 142 mg
Food Exchanges: ½ Milk, ½ Meat

51% calorie reduction from traditional recipe

Chunky Spiced Applesauce

3½ pounds tart cooking apples (about 8 large), peeled and chopped
½ cup water
7¼ teaspoons Equal® Measure™ or 24 packets Equal® sweetener or 1 cup Equal® Spoonful™
½ teaspoon ground cinnamon
¼ teaspoon ground nutmeg
1 to 2 dashes salt

● Combine apples and water in large saucepan; heat to boiling. Reduce heat and simmer, covered, until apples are tender, 20 to 25 minutes.

● Mash apples coarsely with fork; stir in Equal®, cinnamon, nutmeg and salt. Serve warm, or refrigerate and serve chilled.

Makes 10 (½-cup) servings

Note: Amount of Equal® may vary depending on the tartness of the apples.

Nutrition information per serving:

Calories: 104, Protein: 0 g, Carbohydrates: 27 g, Fat: 1 g, Cholesterol: 0 mg, Sodium: 14 mg
Food Exchanges: 1½ Fruit

40% calorie reduction from traditional recipe

Grandma's Apple Crisp

¾ **cup apple juice**
3½ **teaspoons Equal® Measure™ or 12 packets Equal®
      sweetener or ½ cup Equal® Spoonful™**
1 **tablespoon cornstarch**
1 **teaspoon grated lemon peel**
4 **cups sliced peeled apples**
   Crispy Topping (recipe follows)

● Combine apple juice, Equal®, cornstarch and lemon peel in
medium saucepan; add apples and heat to boiling. Reduce heat
and simmer, uncovered, until juice is thickened and apples
begin to lose their crispness, about 5 minutes.

● Arrange apples in 8-inch square baking pan; sprinkle Crispy
Topping over apples. Bake in preheated 400°F oven until
topping is browned and apples are tender, about 25 minutes.
Serve warm.   *Makes 6 servings*

Crispy Topping

¼ **cup all-purpose flour**
2½ **teaspoons Equal® Measure™ or 8 packets Equal®
      sweetener or ⅓ cup Equal® Spoonful™**
1 **teaspoon ground cinnamon**
½ **teaspoon ground nutmeg**
3 **dashes ground allspice**
4 **tablespoons cold margarine, cut into pieces**
¼ **cup quick-cooking oats**
¼ **cup unsweetened flaked coconut***

● Combine flour, Equal® and spices in small bowl; cut in
margarine with pastry blender until mixture resembles coarse
crumbs. Stir in oats and coconut.

*Unsweetened coconut can be purchased in health food stores.

Nutrition information per serving:
Calories: 196, Protein: 2 g, Carbohydrates: 27 g, Fat: 10 g,
Cholesterol: 0 mg, Sodium: 91 mg
Food Exchanges: 1½ Bread, 2 Fat

39% calorie reduction from traditional recipe

Grandma's Apple Crisp

French Vanilla Freeze

**10¾ teaspoons Equal® Measure™ or 36 packets Equal®
sweetener or 1½ cups Equal® Spoonful™**
2 tablespoons cornstarch
1 piece vanilla bean (2 inches)
⅛ teaspoon salt
2 cups skim milk
2 tablespoons margarine
1 cup real liquid egg product
1 teaspoon vanilla

● Combine Equal®, cornstarch, vanilla bean and salt in medium saucepan; stir in milk and margarine. Heat to boiling over medium-high heat, whisking constantly. Boil until thickened, whisking constantly, about 1 minute.

● Whisk about 1 cup milk mixture into egg product in small bowl; whisk egg mixture back into milk mixture in saucepan. Cook over very low heat, whisking constantly, 30 to 60 seconds. Remove from heat and stir in vanilla. Let cool; remove vanilla bean. Refrigerate until chilled, about 1 hour.

● Freeze mixture in ice cream maker according to manufacturer's directions. Pack into freezer container and freeze until firm, 8 hours or overnight. Before serving, let stand at room temperature until slightly softened, about 15 minutes.

Makes 6 (½-cup) servings

Nutrition information per serving:
Calories: 134, Protein: 8 g, Carbohydrates: 13 g, Fat: 5 g, Cholesterol: 2 mg, Sodium: 205 mg
Food Exchanges: 1 Milk, 1 Fat

64% calorie reduction from traditional recipe

Creamy Rice Pudding

    2 cups water
    1 cinnamon stick, broken into pieces
    1 cup converted rice
    4 cups skim milk
    ¼ teaspoon salt
    7¼ teaspoons Equal® Measure™ or 24 packets Equal®
        sweetener or 1 cup Equal® Spoonful™
    3 egg yolks
    2 egg whites
    1 teaspoon vanilla
    ¼ cup raisins
    Ground cinnamon and nutmeg

● Heat water and cinnamon stick to boiling in large saucepan; stir in rice. Reduce heat and simmer, covered, until rice is tender and water is absorbed, 20 to 25 minutes. Discard cinnamon stick.

● Stir in milk and salt; heat to boiling. Reduce heat and simmer, covered, until mixture starts to thicken, about 15 to 20 minutes, stirring frequently. (Milk will not be absorbed and pudding will thicken when it cools.) Remove from heat and cool 1 to 2 minutes; stir in Equal®.

● Beat egg yolks, egg whites and vanilla in small bowl until blended. Stir about ½ cup rice mixture into egg mixture; stir back into saucepan. Cook over low heat, stirring constantly, 1 to 2 minutes. Stir in raisins.

● Spoon pudding into serving bowl; sprinkle with cinnamon and nutmeg. Serve warm or at room temperature.

Makes 6 (⅔-cup) servings

Nutrition information per serving:
Calories: 244, Protein: 11 g, Carbohydrates: 43 g, Fat: 3 g,
Cholesterol: 109 mg, Sodium: 200 mg
Food Exchanges: 1 Milk, 2 Bread, ½ Fat

49% calorie reduction from traditional recipe

Fresh Plum Cobbler

½ cup water
5½ teaspoons Equal® Measure™ or 18 packets Equal®
    sweetener or ¾ cup Equal® Spoonful™
1½ tablespoons cornstarch
1 teaspoon lemon juice
4 cups sliced pitted plums
¼ teaspoon ground nutmeg
¼ teaspoon ground allspice
1 cup all-purpose flour
1½ teaspoons baking powder
1¾ teaspoons Equal® Measure™ or 6 packets Equal®
    sweetener or ¼ cup Equal® Spoonful™
½ teaspoon salt
3 tablespoons cold margarine, cut into pieces
½ cup skim milk

● Combine water, 5½ teaspoons Equal® Measure™ or 18 packets Equal® sweetener or ¾ cup Equal® Spoonful™, cornstarch and lemon juice in large saucepan; add plums and heat to boiling. Boil, stirring constantly, until thickened, about 1 minute. Stir in nutmeg and ⅛ teaspoon allspice. Pour mixture into ungreased 1½-quart casserole.

● Combine flour, baking powder, 1¾ teaspoons Equal® Measure™ or 6 packets Equal® sweetener or ¼ cup Equal® Spoonful™, salt and remaining ⅛ teaspoon allspice in medium bowl; cut in margarine with pastry blender until mixture resembles coarse crumbs. Stir in milk, forming dough. Spoon dough into 6 mounds on fruit.

● Bake cobbler, uncovered, in preheated 400°F oven until topping is golden brown, about 25 minutes. Serve warm.

Makes 6 servings

Nutrition information per serving:
Calories: 195, Protein: 3 g, Carbohydrates: 32 g, Fat: 6 g, Cholesterol: 0 mg, Sodium: 378 mg
Food Exchanges: 1 Fruit, 1 Bread, 1 Fat

38% calorie reduction from traditional recipe

EQUAL®

Index